POJO'S UNOFFICIAL

ADVANCED

NEW

POKÉMON GO®

The **BEST TIPS** and **STRATEGIES** for the **WORLD'S HOTTEST GAME!**

T0164417

This book is available in quantity at special discounts for your group or organization. For further information, contact:

Triumph Books LLC
814 North Franklin Street
Chicago, Illinois 60610
Phone: (312) 337-0747
www.triumphbooks.com

Printed in U.S.A.
ISBN: 978-1-62937-420-8

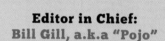

Editor in Chief:
Bill Gill, a.k.a "Pojo"

Graphics Designer:
Phil Deppen

Writers:
Scott Gerhardt,
Adam Motin, Amy Gill,
and Bill Gill

Cover design:
Preston Pisellini

From Pojo

A Great Game for the 20th Anniversary of Pokémon!

Pokémon started in Japan in 1996, and came to the U.S. in 1998. I have played a lot of Pokémon games over the last 18 years, starting with Pokémon Red and the Base Set Trading Card Game. And to be honest, I'm really enjoying Pokémon GO in Pokémon Year 20!

According to the game, I have walked over 100 miles while playing Pokémon GO. I have spent more time outdoors, met a lot of wonderful people, and visited some new and wonderful places I would have never sought out. My kids and I all play the game, and go on family hunts together, which are great!

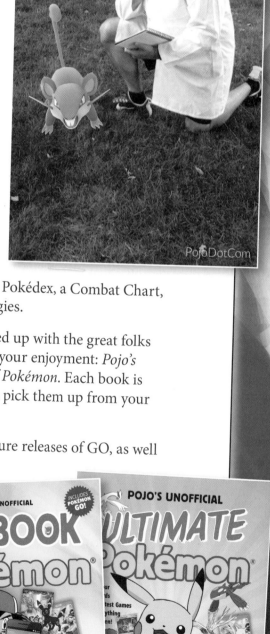

PojoDotCom

The Pojo team has put a lot time and research into this new GO book for you. We think it's an invaluable tool for learning the intricacies of the game, and deciding what to do with all those Pokémon you've caught. You will find a full Pokédex, a Combat Chart, Move Charts, Top 20 Lists, and a plethora of advanced strategies.

And, to celebrate the 20th anniversary of Pokémon, we teamed up with the great folks at Triumph Books and created two more Pokémon books for your enjoyment: *Pojo's Unofficial Ultimate Pokémon* and *Pojo's Unofficial Big Book of Pokémon*. Each book is unique and makes great reading for Pokémon lovers! You can pick them up from your favorite bookstore.

I'm looking forward to the next generation of Pokémon in future releases of GO, as well as the next generation of Pokémon games from the Pokémon Company. Enjoy the book, and happy hunting!

Pojo

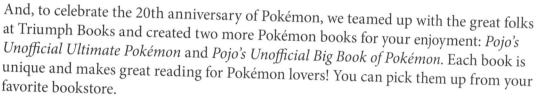

P.S. Feel free to contact us at www.pojo.com if you have questions or want to share something with us.

WHAT'S INSIDE

INTRODUCTION

Pokémon GO is an "Augmented Reality" game, blending the real world and the Pokémon world into a playable adventure on your mobile device.

Players visit real-world locations in order to discover Pokémon, catch Pokémon, battle Pokémon trainers at Gyms, and look for Pokémon-related items. Pokémon GO is a free-to-play mobile app for iPhone and Android devices. It is what many people call a "freemium" game. It's completely "free" to download and play. You also use the "premium" option to buy in-game currency called Pokécoins. Pokécoins can be used to purchase additional Pokéballs and other items. Pokécoins are not needed in order to play Pokémon GO. In fact, the game is thoroughly enjoyable without spending a dime.

Pokémon GO works using GPS, and identifying your current real-world location. The GPS puts your avatar onto a cartoony version of Google Maps. Your avatar is a cartoony version of you. The maps are extremely detailed, showing roads, buildings, houses, rivers, parks, signs, ponds, lakes, monuments, etc.

The next requirement in the game is that you actually go outside and move! The map will show you nearby Pokémon to find, Pokéstops you should visit, and Gyms where you can battle. It's all pretty amazing if you ask us. And it's your job to "catch 'em all" and "visit 'em all"!

So...What Are Pokémon?

We've been Pokémon experts at Pojo since 1998. We started a Pokémon website, www.pojo.com, 18 years ago, and we still maintain it on a daily basis. We also realize that this might be the first time some of you are playing a Pokémon-themed game. So here is a little Pokémon history lesson.

Satoshi Tajiri of Japan is credited with creating Pocket Monsters / Pokémon. He loved catching insects and tadpoles as a kid in the suburbs of Tokyo. He also loved arcade games. As a young adult, he started a Gaming Magazine called *GameFreak*. He met many game designers through his video game publication. When he first saw the Nintendo Game Boy system and Link Cable, he imagined insects traveling across the link cable to other Game Boys. He thought he

could make a video game where people collected bugs and critters and traded them across the Game Boy Cable. He pitched his idea to friends at Nintendo. Nintendo funded his project.

Satoshi Tajari spent six years developing the games that would ultimately become Pocket Monsters Green and Pocket Monsters Red in Japan. Red and Green were released in 1996, and Pocket Monsters was a huge success in Japan. Due to trademark issues, the name was shortened to "Pokémon" for the North American release.

Pokémon Red and Blue were released

Pokémon Snap

Catching Pokémon is a Snap!

In the Pokémon RPGs, you are a trainer trying to catch a variety of pocket monsters (Pokémon) that appear in the game. Once caught, Pokémon can be added to your party and trained to assist you. The longer you train Pokémon, the more attacks they learn, and the stronger they become.

Various versions of Pokémon Red and Blue have been released over the years, amassing over 57 million units of sales. In total, the Pokémon franchise has sold over 279 million copies of Pokémon-themed games!

Pokémon Snap

An old Pokémon video game that is somewhat similar to Pokémon GO is a game called Pokémon Snap. Pokémon Snap was released on the Nintendo 64 in 1999. In Pokémon Snap, you played a Pokémon photographer named Todd Snap.

simultaneously in North America in 1998. They are the granddaddies of all Pokémon games. The games seem to be simple children's games, but they are actually very deep Role Playing Games (RPGs). The games feature a ton of strategy and a dynamic storyline.

The premise of this game was that you rolled through various Pokémon environments in a cart on a track,

and took photographs of Pokémon for Professor Oak. We know it sounds lame, but it was a ton of fun and extremely addictive.

After each Rail Ride, Professor Oak graded your photos. You kept trying to photograph all the Pokémon you could and tried to get better shots on each pass. You had some items at your disposal to interact with the Pokémon environment while riding along, like a flute, apples, and Pester Balls. People loved Pokémon Snap. You could even take your game cartridge down to the local Blockbuster video store and print your pictures out as stickers.

Pokéfans over the years dreamed of a real-world version of Pokémon Snap, and started making YouTube videos merging the Pokémon world into the real world. Some of these videos are extremely creative if you want to Google them.

Pokémon Dream Radar

Next there came a little-known game called Pokémon Dream Radar. This game was released in 2012, and was the first Pokémon game to use Augmented Reality (AR).

You used the camera on your 3DS as a view finder and walked around your house. You also used the 3DS system as a radar. Dream Clouds would sometimes appear, partially blocking your view on the screen. You would clear the Dream Clouds off your screen like a first-person shooter. The cleared Dream Clouds would often reveal Pokémon to capture inside your house. This game was a fun little diversion and only cost about $3.

Ingress

In the fall of 2012, Niantic and Google created an app called Ingress for Android phones. The game is still played by fans today. Ingress is an AR, multiplayer, online-location-based game. The game has a story line

based in science fiction. You pick one of two sides: the Enlightened or the Resistance. The game plays in real time and in the real world.

Ingress is like a giant game of Capture the Flag. You attack enemy portals, protect your own portals, collect Exotic Matter, and a whole lot more. One cool aspect about Ingress is that players can suggest Portal locations—statues, buildings, paintings, tourist spots, etc. Niantic would evaluate the suggestions, and add them into the game.

The game has been installed on over 10 million Android devices.

Pojo Note: Many of the Portals and Exotic Matter sites in Ingress serve as Pokéstops and Pokémon spawning points. Some clever Pokémon collectors have fired up Ingress on their phones to find places to catch rare Pokémon in Pokémon GO! Each game is sharing the same data!

Enter Pokémon GO!

In 2015, Nintendo and The Pokémon Company Group announced that they would work with Niantic to create Pokémon GO, a global location-based game where you would go into the real world and catch Pokémon. It was a plan to marry Niantic's Ingress gaming engine with the awesomeness of the Pokémon franchise.

Pokémon GO was released in the United States on July 6, 2016. Within 10 days, it was the biggest mobile game in U.S. history, passing Candy Crush's 2013 popularity in number of active users.

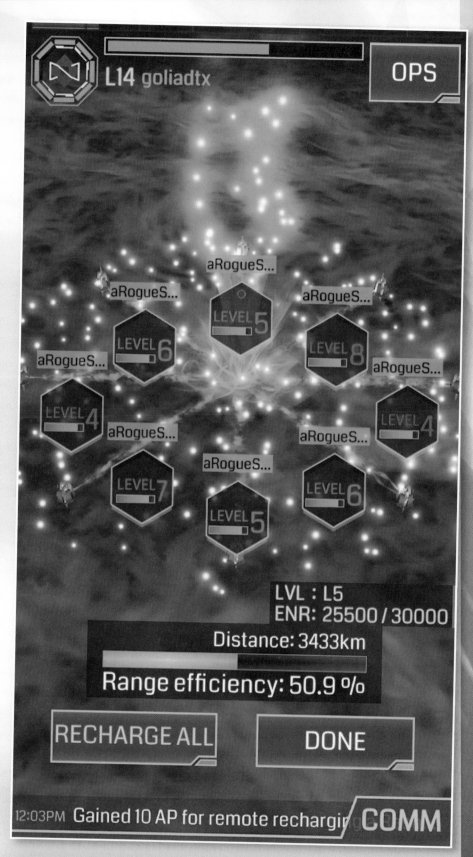

As we write this guide, Pokémon GO has been downloaded over 500 million times. The game is being played in North America, South America, Europe, Australia, New Zealand, Japan and Hong Kong, and Southeast Asia.

What makes Pokémon GO so appealing?

One reason is that Pokémon GO does a pretty good job of replicating the core components of the Pokémon RPG franchise in the real world. You see

Pokémon and you catch Pokémon in the wild.

Another appeal of Pokémon GO is the social impact. You can play this game while you are out with friends and family. You can go for walks together, catch Pokémon together, and share the same gaming experience. You can attack Gyms as a team and feel a sense of joint accomplishment.

Another appeal is the power of nostalgia. Many of the people playing Pokémon GO are in their 20s, 30s,

and 40s. In 1998, they were in elementary school, or high school, or college when they were playing the original Pokémon games. They know all of the original 151 Pokémon in the game, and they want to "catch 'em all" again!

Another reason is that Pokémon GO gives you something to do while you walk and exercise. If you are going for a walk around the park, you might as well catch a few Pokémon to work your brain as well. You can get lost in the gaming, and completely forget that you've walked thousands of steps.

And yet another appeal is that Pokémon GO is completely FREE! You don't have to spend a penny to enjoy Pokémon GO!

Enter this advanced guide!

We know that Pokémon GO now has a huge audience, and that some of our readers have no idea what Pokémon is, or what a Pokédex is. Some of you might not have a clue of what to do at a Pokémon Gym. You might not have any idea what a Pokémon Combat Chart is, or which Pokémon are best to use to attack. Many old-school Pokémon players know this stuff by heart from years of Pokémon gaming experience, but others simply do not. So we've created this guide to walk you through everything you need to become a Pokémon GO master!

You don't get an instruction manual with Pokémon GO, but you have one now! We'll walk you through catching your first Pokémon, to evolving your first Pokémon, to taking down a Gym Leader. We explain everything that happens within the game. There is also a detailed Pokédex to help you determine which of your Pokémon are the best.

If you haven't tried Pokémon GO yet, there is no need to be intimidated. Download the app, read our guide, and "catch 'em all!"

SAFETY FIRST!

You probably have heard stories about people getting injured while playing Pokémon GO. Some folks have walked into traffic. Others have crashed their cars playing while driving. And some people have actually walked off cliffs! It's easy to get caught up playing Pokémon GO, but you still need to pay attention to your environment. Stop walking if you are searching for Pokémon. Stop walking if you are catching a Pokémon. If you need to look at your screen, you should stop what you are doing and just be safe.

You're going too fast!

Pokémon GO should not be played while driving.

I'M A PASSENGER

Safety can mean many things though, besides not walking off a bridge:

✔ First and foremost—always be aware of your surroundings! Keep to areas you know are safe for playing Pokémon GO, and pay attention to strangers around you. You may be hunting Pokémon, but someone there might be hunting wallets and purses. If you are going into a strange area, make sure you walk with friends.

✔ If you're going on a long hunt in the sun, apply sunscreen. If it's winter, consider touchscreen gloves to protect your hands.

✔ If you're crossing the street, make sure you pay attention to the cars—do not assume drivers will see you and stop.

✔ Don't enter private property. Don't assume a property owner is okay with you hunting Pokémon on their front lawn.

✔ Make sure don't get dehydrated if you are going on a long hunt. Bring drinks and snacks.

✔ Always wear bright colors at night. If other people can't see you, they can't avoid you.

✔ Have backup battery power. The last thing you want is a dead cell phone when you run into an emergency.

And last but not least—NEVER play while driving a car or riding a bike. No Pokémon is worth it!

DON'T DRIVE DISTRACTED
#PlaySafe

HOW TO GET PIKACHU AS YOUR STARTING POKÉMON!

In the Pokémon Anime, Ash starts with Pikachu. So the creators of Pokémon GO put a little Easter Egg in the game so you can start with Pikachu, too.

We are sharing this information with you early in the book because it's very easy to miss. This might be beyond folks at this late stage, but maybe you're thinking of starting a second account? Or, maybe you're helping someone start their first account?

Okay, first things first. You have to be starting the game at the very beginning. When you start playing Pokémon GO, you are presented with three choices of Pokémon: Charmander, Squirtle, and Bulbasaur. These are the same three choices players had at the beginning of Pokémon Red and Blue back in 1998.

You have to ignore these Pokémon! Don't catch any of them. Instead, head outside and go on a nice long walk. Walking in circles won't count. GO's internal GPS needs you to walk far away from your starting point. After about 200 yards or so, the three starting Pokémon will pop back up in a new place tempting you to catch them. You have to ignore them again, and keep walking farther away. After another 200 yards or so, they will pop back up again. You still have to ignore them, and keep walking. You need to keep this up. Rinse and repeat about four times in total.

Eventually, Pikachu will pop in with Charmander, Squirtle, and Bulbasaur, and you can catch Pikachu!

We started a new account just to test this out, and it works great! This is not a myth! We went for a walk and it took only a half block for Pikachu to pop up. One thing we also learned is that if you ignore Pikachu and keep walking, Pikachu will not pop up the next time. We were goofing around taking screen captures and forgot to capture Pikachu. The next time only the three main starters popped up. We had to ignore the main starters four more times before Pikachu eventually popped up again! Phew!

Good luck capturing your very own Pikachu!

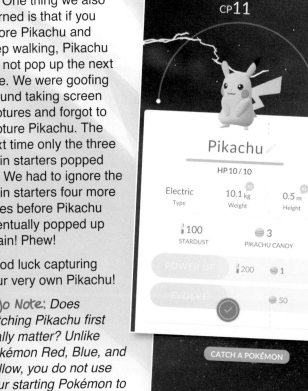

Pojo Note: Does catching Pikachu first really matter? Unlike Pokémon Red, Blue, and Yellow, you do not use your starting Pokémon to actually battle in Pokémon GO. Capturing one of these four Pokémon is more of a tutorial to get you on your way. All four of these Pokémon are uncommon to find in the wild. You will need to capture a whole bunch to fully evolve them. Evolving Pikachu to final form is easiest. Evolving Pikachu to Raichu will probably happen before you can evolve any of the other starters into their Stage 2 forms. Raichu will be helpful early in Gym battles, so you might want to consider getting Pikachu as your first Pokémon. Or, pick your favorite. If you really want a Charizard, take a Charmander!

MAP VIEW SCREEN

The Map View Screen is where you will spend most of your time, so you should get comfortable with it.

The avatar walking in the middle is you! The game map always tries to keep you centered and walking in the direction you are actually moving in the real world. The map view GPS might show you in the wrong location when you first start the game, but the game's GPS will eventually match your real-world location. Tall buildings and trees can throw off the GPS at times.

The map you see is the real world around you, taken directly from Google Maps. The compass is in the upper right corner. The red arrow always points north, so it's easy to always know which way you are going. Clicking on the compass toggles the viewing direction in Map View. You can switch between a north-viewing direction and auto-rotation, which follows your viewing direction. You can also slide your finger across the map to change your perspective, and you can pinch the screen in or out to zoom the map in or out.

The pulsing circle under your avatar is your "Action Circle" or "Action Radius." To interact with anything in the game, you must bring it within your Action Circle by walking to it. The maximum distance it reaches is roughly 120 feet.

In the bottom right corner is your Nearby Screen, showing you the three nearest wild Pokémon to you. Touching it brings up the full Nearby Screen, which we will discuss elsewhere in this book.

The bottom left corner has your profile icon, your name, and your level. The level bar fills as you get closer to your next level. Tapping the profile icon will take you to your Progress and Achievements Screen.

Last is the Pokéball in the bottom center. Touching it will take you to the Main Menu.

The map might also display Pokéstops and Gyms, which we will cover in the next few pages.

PROGRESS AND ACHIEVEMENTS SCREEN

The Progress and Achievements Screen is a great place to keep up with how you are progressing in the game.

Your name is at the top and your full avatar below. You can swipe left and right to rotate your avatar around and see your backpack.

Under that is your level, plus how much XP (experience) you have, and how much XP you need to reach the next level.

The gold Pikachu button on the bottom left shows you how many Pokécoins you have. Clicking on it will take you to the Shop. Your start date and the Team you chose is also shown.

The X button will return you to the Map View Screen. The blue button with the white lines on the bottom right will take you to your Journal and allow you to re-customize your avatar.

Your Journal will show you the last 50 things that have happened to you in the game, such as Pokémon caught, Pokémon missed, Eggs hatched, Items you received at Pokéstops, etc. This is a good place to go if you missed something occurring in the game. We've had Eggs hatch that we didn't see animation for. Or you can check if you actually received items from Pokéstops.

You can also scroll down further and see all of your Achievements. There are a lot of fun awards here.

You'll get awards for how far you've walked, how many Pokémon you have in your Pokédex, how many total Pokémon you have caught, and how many Pokémon you have evolved. You can see how many Eggs you've hatched, how many Pokéstops you've visited, how many Gym battles you have won, and how many times you have trained at your own Gym.

The next 14 Awards are all for catching certain kinds of Pokémon, and the last two are specifically for catching CP 10 Ratatas for Youngster and how many total Pikachus you have.

Everything you could ever want to know (or brag to your friends) about can be found here on this screen!

This book is not sponsored, endorsed by, or otherwise affiliated with any companies or the products featured in the book. This is not an official publication.

15

SIGHTINGS SCREEN

When Pokémon Go was first released on July 6, 2016, players could hunt down Pokémon using the Nearby Screen, which worked like the classic kids' game "Hot & Cold." Pokémon on the Nearby Screen had little footprints over their heads representing how far they were away from you:

- No footsteps meant a Pokémon was 0m to 40m away
- One footstep meant the Pokémon was 40m to 75m away
- Two footsteps meant the Pokémon was 75m to 150m away
- Three footsteps meant the Pokémon was 150m to 225m away.

If you were tracking a Paras in a big field and it was two footprints away, you would pick a direction to walk to hunt it. If it switched to three footprints away, you knew you were going the wrong way. It was fun and it worked.

But a few weeks after launching, Niantic removed the footprints over the Pokémons' heads on the Nearby Screen. They claimed that it was causing too much stress on their servers. The screen was renamed the Sightings Screen, and just showed you Pokémon within 200 meters of your location. The Pokemon order meant nothing whatsoever. This left players with no way to efficiently track Pokémon. Technically-gifted fans wrote programs and apps, such as PokeVision, PokeMesh, FastPoke, etc., as a stopgap measure. Niantic tried to shut down these programs as they too place demands on their servers. Niantic even banned players suspected of using them! This was bad as many of these players were paying customers

just trying to figure out how to hunt down Pokémon.

Niantic promised to repair/replace the broken Nearby Screen and rolled out a beta in San Francisco in early August 2016. In the beta version, the Nearby Screen shows Pokémon near Pokéstops if they're actually near those landmarks. But if a Pokémon is not near a landmark, you're still out of luck. You have no idea what direction to walk in.

As we write this book, there is still no working Pokémon tracking system in the game—outside of San Francisco. Most players are just hoping they blindly stumble into a wild Pokémon, while others are using one of the Pokémon tracking programs that Niantic frowns upon. We sincerely hope Niantic has something in place as you read this, because this function has been broken for far too long.

BUDDY POKÉMON

In mid-September 2016, the Buddy Pokémon option was added to Pokémon GO.

You can pick your favorite Pokémon from your collection to become your buddy, opening up unique in-game rewards and experiences. Buddy Pokémon appear alongside your avatar on your profile screen, adding helpful bonuses such as awarding Candy for walking together. You also have the ability to change your Buddy Pokémon at any time.

Unfortunately, your Buddy Pokémon does not follow your avatar around like Pikachu does in Pokémon Yellow. We hope Niantic will add that in a future patch.

When you assign a Pokémon as your buddy, it will collect Candy for you. If you assign Pikachu as your buddy, it will collect Pikachu Candy. Rattata will pick up Rattata Candy. Evolved Pokémon will pick up the base Candy for their line (for example, Blastoise will pick up Squirtle Candy).

You have to do a lot of walking to get Candy, so be prepared for the grind. Weaker Pokémon lines such as Caterpie, Weedle, Pidgey, and Rattata will give you one candy for each km you walk. The Charmander, Squirtle, and Bulbasaur type lines will give you about one candy for every 2km you walk. And rarer Pokémon near the end of the Pokédex, such as Lapras, Snorlax, Vaporeon, and Dragonite, will give you one candy for every 3km you walk.

So if you choose Snorlax as your buddy, you will have to walk 1.9 miles to get one piece of Snorlax Candy. That's a lot of walking! But considering how rare some of these Pokémon are in the wild, we think it's a great idea to help you power these guys up for Gym battles!

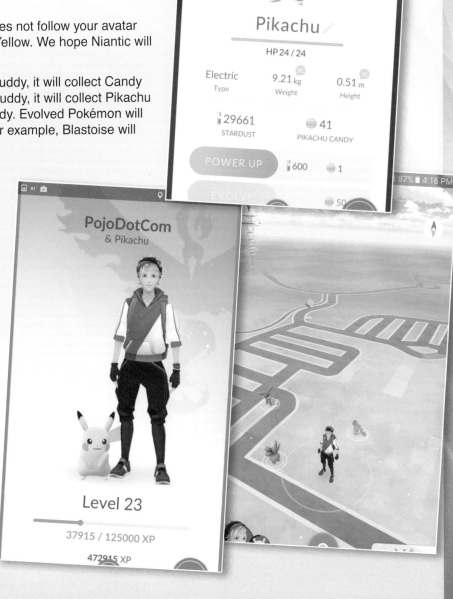

POKÉDEX AND POKÉMON SCREENS

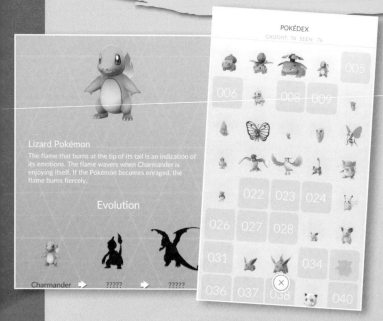

also show you what type of Pokémon it is, such as Fire, Psychic, or Ground. It will also provide you with a little more information about that Pokémon. In addition, if the Pokémon has an Evolution, you can see it there. If you have not seen the Evolutions, though, it won't tell you anything about them. For example, if you have seen Charmander, but not Charmeleon or Charizard, then you will see question marks and shadows for those two.

If you want to see exactly how many Pidgeys or Ratatas you have seen, this is where you can find out!

We also have a huge Pokédex in the back of the book for you!

The Pokédex Screen

The Pokédex is where you can learn all about the Pokémon you have caught.

Each Pokémon corresponds to an individual number. This goes all the way back to the Pokémon Red and Blue! There were 151 Pokémon in Red and Blue, matching the number in Pokémon GO. These original 151 Pokémon are considered Generation I Pokémon. The Gold and Silver games added more Pokémon, which were considered Generation II. This has gone on for 20 years, and we're up to Generation VII Pokémon now.

If you encounter a Pokémon at least once, there will be a shadow of that Pokémon in the Pokédex where it belongs. See #35 on the example Pokédex Screen? We have seen Clefairy, but haven't caught Clefairy. The Pokédex won't tell you much except the number and name, and how many times you've seen it. If you have caught that Pokémon, you get to see a lot more information.

You can also see the numbers in the Pokédex of Pokémon you haven't seen yet. On the example screen, we haven't seen #005 or #006, which are Charmeleon and Charizard.

The Pokédex will show you how many of a particular Pokémon you have seen and caught, as well an average weight and height for the Pokémon. It will

The Main Pokémon Screen

The Pokémon Screen is one of the most useful screens in the game! You can see all the Pokémon you own, and sort them in many different ways. There is also a tab in the upper-right-hand corner that takes you to your Eggs Screen.

In the bottom-right-hand corner of your screen, you will see a "#" button. This allows you to sort your Pokémon in various ways. You have six options when sorting Pokémon:

- First is by "Recent," so you can tell what you have caught lately. Also, if you opened an Egg

and didn't realize it, the recent screen can help you figure that out! We also find this handy for calculating IVs on new Pokémon (we'll cover this later in the book).

- Next is by "Favorite." All those Pokémon you "starred" previously can now be sorted together, so you can see them all at the same time.

- Sorting by "Number" will show you the Pokémon in the order they are in the Pokédex.

- If you want to know who your biggest Pokémon are, you can sort by "HP"—Hit Points. This might come in handy if you want to put your beefiest Pokémon in a Gym.

- If you just want to sort them "Alphabetically," you can do that, too. This makes it easier to "clean up" your Pokémon Bags and trade Pokémon you no longer need to Professor Willow for Candy.

- Finally, you can sort by "CP," which will rank your Pokémon by their "Combat Power." This is handy for Gym battles.

The Individual Pokémon Screen

When you tap on an individual Pokémon, it will bring up a screen for that specific Pokémon. You can find out all kinds of information about each Pokémon: CP (Combat Power), HP (Hit Points), the Type of Pokémon it is, as well as its height and weight. You can also find out how much total Stardust you have and how much Pokémon Candy you have. There is a pencil next to each Pokémon's name. You can rename your Pokémon here by tapping the pencil image.

Candy is used to both power up and evolve Pokémon. Candy is specific to each line of Pokémon. For example, you can evolve Dratini into Dragonair, and then Dragonair into Dragonite. Both of these evolutions require Dratini Candy. Candy is named after the lowest evolution in the chain. You will need 25 Dratini Candy to evolve Dratini into Dragonair, and you will need 100 Dratini Candy to evolve Dragonair into Dragonite. This is discussed more later in this book.

When you scroll down, you will see the Pokémon's two attacks and its attack strength. The first attack is the Base Attack. The second attack is its Special (Charged) Attack. The number after each attack is

the Attack Power. Power is simply a base statistic, not the damage it does. Pokémon attacks are effected by the Attack Power, the Pokémon's Level, and the Pokémon's Base Attack Power. Don't let the Power of a particular move fool you, though. Generally, moves with higher power will have slower attack speeds. The attack Speed and Damage Per Second (DPS) formulas in Pokémon can get pretty complicated. You can find them online if you're interested.

Lastly, in the bottom-right-hand corner is a button that brings up options for Favorite, Appraise, and Transfer Pokémon.

Transfer allows you to sell Pokémon to Professor Willow for some Pokémon Candy. We discuss this in a later chapter. Appraise will bring your team's Leader, who will rate your individual Pokémon. No two Pokémon, even with the same name, are equal. We discuss this later in the book as well.

Clicking on Favorite will put a Yellow Star in the upper-right-hand corner of the Pokémon Screen. Besides the cool star, it also protects you from accidentally transferring a great Pokémon to Professor Willow in exchange for Candy. Always "favorite" really good Pokémon to protect them!

EGG SCREEN

The Eggs on this screen are Pokémon that have not hatched yet. You nurture/hatch them by putting them in Incubators and walking with them. You can hold up to nine eggs at a time. For each Egg, you will have three different distances marked—2km, 5km, and 10km. Each distance refers to how far you have to walk the Eggs to hatch them.

To hatch an Egg, you have to put it into an Incubator. Just tap on an Egg, and it will ask if you want to incubate it. (You can also find your Incubators on your Items page). An Incubator can only hold one Egg at a time. You have one Infinity Incubator, marked with a "∞," that you can use unlimited times. (That is the orange Incubator.) To incubate and hatch multiple Eggs at the same time, you would need more Incubators. You will get free Incubators when you reach Levels 6, 10, 15, and 20. You can also purchase additional Incubators in the Shop. Aside from the Infinity Incubator, the other Incubators in the game can only be used three times.

Once you have walked the distance required to hatch an Egg, the Hatching Screen will show up and hatch the Egg. The longer the distance, the better chance you have of getting a rare and powerful Pokémon, but nothing is guaranteed. You can sometimes get strong Pokémon from a 2km Egg and sometimes weaker Pokémon from a 10km Egg—you never know until they hatch. Once an Egg hatches, you will eventually get a replacement from a Pokéstop.

Unfortunately, you can't get rid of Eggs you don't want—you have to hatch them. So, if you have a bunch of 2km and 5km Eggs and you want a 10km Egg, your only choice is to hatch the lower ones and hope to

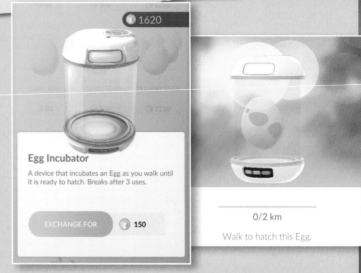

get a 10km Egg from the next stop. Eggs also come with a lot of Candy, so it's a great way to power up a Pokémon fast!

We recommend that you always use your Infinity Incubator for 2km eggs first. Use your limited-use incubators for 5km and 10km eggs. This way you will be getting 15km to 30km of walking with the limited-use Incubators, as opposed to just 6km of walking. Any time the Infinity Incubator is empty, toss the lowest km Egg into it.

If you decide to purchase an Incubator from the Shop, it will cost you 150 Pokécoins. These incubators can only be used three times and then they break. A Pokécoin is equal to about 1 cent in U.S. dollars. If you are going to spend real money in this game, this isn't a bad way to go, especially if you're enjoying the game.

Egg Hatching Walking Tips:

Make sure you have the Pokémon GO app open while you walk. Kilometers walked when the Pokémon GO app is closed will not count toward hatching your Eggs.

Walking on a treadmill won't cut it. You need to walk outside. Pokémon GO tracks distance traveled with GPS, not the pedometer function on your phone.

The maximum speed you can travel to hatch an Egg is about 6.5 mph. If you are riding a bike, skateboarding, running, or rollerblading any faster than that, the Egg hatching will not count your travel accurately.

WHAT'S INSIDE AN EGG?

We told you all about Pokémon Eggs and how to hatch them. And now you're probably wondering, "What's inside Pokémon Eggs?"

Well, you will get a Pokémon, some XP, some Candy, and some Stardust. Based on reports from around the globe, these are the Pokémon you can find in each type of Egg.

2km Pokémon Eggs:

Bulbasaur, Charmander, Squirtle, Caterpie, Weedle, Pidgey, Rattata, Spearow, Pikachu, Clefairy, Jigglypuff, Zubat, Geodude, Magikarp

5km Pokémon Eggs:

Any of the 2km Pokémon can hatch from a 5km Egg, plus:

Ekans, Sandshrew, Nidoran♀, Nidoran♂, Vulpix, Oddish, Paras, Venonat, Diglett, Meowth, Psyduck, Mankey, Growlithe, Poliwag, Abra, Machop, Bellsprout, Tentacool, Ponyta, Slowpoke, Magnemite, Farfetch'd, Doduo, Seel, Grimer, Shellder, Gastly, Drowzee, Krabby, Voltorb, Exeggcute, Cubone, Lickitung, Koffing, Rhyhorn, Tangela, Kangaskhan, Horsea, Goldeen, Staryu, Tauros, Porygon

10km Pokémon Eggs:

Any of the 2km or 5km Pokémon can hatch from a 10km Egg, plus:

Onix, Hitmonlee, Hitmonchan, Chansey, Mr. Mime, Scyther, Jynx, Electabuzz, Magmar, Pinsir, Lapras, Eevee, Omanyte, Kabuto, Aerodactyl, Snorlax, Dratini

Yes, it can be somewhat of a letdown to get 2km Pokémon inside 5km and 10km Eggs. Just be prepared for it! The bright spot is that you still get a lot of XP, Candy, and Stardust! Another bright spot is that the hatched Pokémon will usually have very strong IV characteristics (covered later in the book).

Pojo Note: The Silph Road Folks on the Reddit message boards stated that you cannot get any of the foreign "Regional Pokémon" from outside of your region from a hatched Egg. They have hatched thousands of Eggs and have never seen a foreign Pokémon hatch. So if you live in North America, you cannot hatch a Farfetch'd, Mr. Mime, or Kangaskhan.

POKÉSTOPS

Pokéstops are the "blue cube" locations you see on your Map View Screen. Pokéstops are places in Pokémon GO that allow you to freely collect items like Pokéballs, Razz Berries, Potions, Revives, and even Pokémon Eggs. When you get near a Pokéstop, they turn from blue cubes into blue flat circles resembling Pokéballs. That means you are close enough to interact with them.

Whenever you visit a Pokéstop or even click on it, it will bring up the Pokéstop screen. You can get some good information from this screen.

The top of the screen shows you the name of the Pokéstop. Touching the top of the screen will open a

larger image of the stop, and many have additional information about the stop itself listed there. Since a lot of stops are historical markers or various works of art, this is a neat way to learn more about the area you are hunting in. You might actually get a better appreciation for things you pass all the time and take for granted.

Below the name of the stop is a very small white oval. This is where you would put a Lure Module, or where you will see a Lure Module if one has already been added. By touching the white oval, you can install a module if you are close enough, or it will show you the name of the person who installed the module if one is already there. This gives you a chance to thank him or her if you know who it is. A Lured Pokéstop has pink petals falling over it.

The picture of the Pokéstop is below (in the disc) so you can identify it. Interacting with this disc is how you get supplies. Simply swiping your finger across the screen spins the disc, giving you supplies. You do not have to touch the supplies to get them—they are added automatically to your backpack. Once you interact with a Pokéstop, it will turn from blue to pink. You have to wait at least five minutes to use that Pokéstop again. Spinning Pokéstops will always give you 50 XP, even if your bags are full. So even if you can't collect anything from stops, spin them for the experience alone.

If the stop is too far to interact with, a pink oval will appear under that picture saying "This Pokéstop is too far away," letting you know you need to get closer in order to use it. You usually have to be within about 100 feet of a stop to activate it.

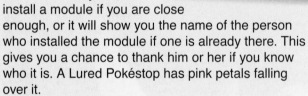

CLOUD GATE

Also known as "The Bean". Sculptor - Anish Kapoor

Some folks have figured out that if you visit 10 unique Pokéstops in a row (no doubling back to a previous stop), you will receive bonus items as well as a guaranteed Egg. Try it!

So, where did all these Pokéstops come from? How did Pokémon GO get all these images?

As we mentioned in the Introduction of this book, Pokémon GO is using data from a game called Ingress created by Niantic in 2012. Ingress had places called Portals that functioned in Ingress somewhat similar to Pokéstops. (We're not going to go into deep comparisons here, but you can research it online.)

When Ingress launched, places like fire stations, museums, village halls, etc. were the main Portals. Niantic then opened up the game and asked its players to submit even more portals. Their criteria for portals was:

- A location with a cool story, a place in history, or educational value
- A cool piece of art or unique architecture
- A hidden gem or hyper-local spot
- Public libraries
- Place of worship

Ingress players could take pictures of any of these locations near them, write a description, and give it a proper title. If Niantic thought it qualified, it was turned into a Portal. (Ingress shut down portal submissions in 2015 due to a tremendous backlog.)

These Portals became Pokéstops and Gyms in Pokémon GO. So if there aren't enough Pokéstops in your area, it's because not enough people in your area where playing Ingress at that time. We assume Niantic will allow Portal/Pokéstop suggestions again, but who knows when?

CATCHING POKÉMON

When you are walking around, you will eventually see Pokémon on your Map View Screen. Simply tap on a Pokémon to try to catch it. When you tap on it, the Catching Pokémon screen pops up.

You will see the Pokémon with its name and CP right above it. If you see "???" over its head, it means it has a higher CP than any other Pokémon you have caught. In the bottom center of the screen, you will see the Pokéball you are going to toss at it, as well as how many Pokéballs you have. This screen gives you other options as well.

At the top left, there is an icon of a man running. This button lets you run away from the Pokémon and stop trying to catch it. This can be handy if you are running out of Pokéballs and want to save them for more uncommon Pokémon.

In the upper right, there is a toggle button for turning the Augmented Reality option on or off. This is discussed in the next few pages.

At the bottom right, you will see two more icons. The Camera icon allows you to take a picture of your Pokémon. The Backpack icon will allow you to switch Pokéball types or feed the Pokémon a Razz Berry. These are all discussed later in the book.

Once you place your finger on the Pokéball, you will be able to flick the Pokéball up at the Pokémon in order to catch it. This gets easier with practice. Once you've become more experienced, you can get an additional XP bonus by spinning the Pokéball with your finger and tossing a curveball, but this can be tough. You also may get an XP boost depending on the circle around the Pokémon. It will say Nice, Great, or Excellent. Niantic says your chance of catching the Pokémon increases when the circle is at its smallest.

Each Pokémon has different colored "toughness rings" surrounding them as well. These rings represent the catching difficulty: Green = Easy; Yellow = Moderate; Orange= Difficult; Red = A Mighty Foe! Tougher Pokémon will pop out of balls more often. They might even knock down or blow your Pokéballs away. You'll want to use stronger Pokéballs on mightier foes.

When a Pokémon spawns, it is usually available for capture for about 15 minutes. Remember, the Pokémon you see is available for everyone in the area to capture, not just you. It is not first come, first served. So if you see someone else playing the game, you can share information about where Pokémon are.

Pojo Note: Some folks have figured out that if you fire up the Ingress app (that we've discussed a few times already in this book), you can use it to see where Pokémon will spawn in your area. The little white energy dots are known as XM in Ingress. Denser areas of white dots are most likely spawn spots for Pokémon. Pokémon will not spawn in areas with no dots. We've tried this method for finding Pokemon and it has worked great for us.

POKÉBALLS

Pokéballs are the single most important item that you can have in Pokémon GO, and also the item you will run low on the quickest.

When you first start out, you will get plain old Pokéballs, which are just fine. Early on, most Pokémon will not break out of their balls, so normal Pokéballs are up to the task. As you start to level up and encounter Pokémon with higher CP, they will break out of regular Pokéballs more often, and you are going to need stronger Pokéballs.

You will gain access to Great Balls at Level 12. Great Balls have a higher catch rate than regular Pokéballs.

At Level 20 you will gain access to Ultra Balls. These have a higher catch rate than Great Balls.

There are 26 varieties of Pokéballs in the Pokémon RPGs, so maybe more will be introduced into Pokémon GO over time. The most powerful Pokéball in Pokémon is the Master Ball. Master Balls have a 100% capture rate and are best used against the hardest-to find Pokémon (such as Mewtwo, if he ever comes out). Master Balls have not been released as we write this, but we have heard they will eventually be in the game.

Remember, using Razz Berries makes it more likely Pokémon will stay captured as well.

ITEMS
250/350

Poké Ball
x63
A device for catching wild Pokémon. It's thrown like a ball at a Pokémon, comfortably encapsulating its target.

Great Ball
x31
A good, high-performance Poké Ball that provides a higher catch rate than a standard Poké Ball.

Ultra Ball
x13
An ultra-high performance Poké Ball that provides a higher catch rate than a Great Ball.

Charmander / CP ???

AUGMENTED REALITY

We briefly discussed Augmented Reality (AR) earlier in this book. There are a lot of differences between trying to catch a Pokémon with AR on and with AR off.

With AR on, you will see the Pokémon in the real world around you. Moving yourself and the camera around will change where the Pokémon is, possibly even moving them off screen. The Pokémon will be at a fixed GPS point in the real world. If the Pokémon is off screen, arrows will appear on the side telling you which way to turn your camera to see the Pokémon again. You have to hold your phone still to be able to catch Pokémon with the Augmented Reality turned on.

With AR off, the Pokémon will always be in the middle of the screen no matter how you stand or what direction you face. It doesn't even matter if your phone is parallel or perpendicular to the ground. This is helpful if you are near someone's house, so that you won't have to turn the camera toward the house to catch a Pokémon. Otherwise, the home owners might wonder why you're hanging around with a camera near their front door.

Catching with AR on is more fun but also more challenging, so practice with the AR turned off until you get the hang of it.

Turning AR on also creates an opportunity for great pictures. You can take a photograph with a Pokémon standing next to a friend or with a pet. You can also find wacky places to take a picture of Pokémon. Taking Pokémon pictures with the AR on takes some practice, but it can also be a ton of fun.

With time, you'll also get good at toggling that AR switch based on your environment. On this page are two screenshots of Gastly for you: one with the AR on in, and one with the AR off.

REGIONAL POKÉMON

Pokémon GO encourages you to explore your area and catch as many wild Pokémon as possible, but you probably haven't had to travel very far outside your usual neighborhood.

Unfortunately, there is an exception to this rule. As of this writing, there are four wild Pokémon that are specific to certain continents.

- Tauros is only in North America
- Farfetch'd is only in Asia
- Mr. Mime is only in Europe
- Kangaskhan is only in Australia

This is bad news for people who are really trying to catch all the Pokémon in the game. Maybe Niantic wants to encourage world travel? Or maybe they plan to implement Pokémon trading, and get players to socialize with other players from the around the globe when they do travel abroad? We'll have to wait and see how this actually plays out.

At first it was believed that you could hatch Pokémon from other regions from your Pokémon Eggs. But this was recently proved false. Egg hatches of each Pokémon are limited to each continent, too.

At this point in time, it's going to take some extra work to actually catch 'em all!

ITEMS SCREEN

You have somewhat of a magic backpack in Pokémon. Your backpack can hold 350 items! The Items Screen shows you everything inside your backpack.

On the Items Screen, you can see exactly which items you own and how many of each you've acquired. Each item has an explanation of what it is and the inventory count. You also will have a trash can next to each item, allowing you to get rid of items you don't want or don't need.

At the very top of the screen, you'll see how many slots you have used and how many you have left available. If you start to run tight on space, you should trash some stuff to make room for more Pokéballs. We have found that the items we most want to trash are Revives and lower-level Potions. Never trash all of them, though!

If you are near a Gym, you could battle to get rid of Potions and Revives without wasting them.

Never get rid of Incense, Lucky Eggs, Pokéballs, or Lure Modules. These Items are way too useful, and cost Pokécoins to buy.

And don't forget, your Camera and Egg Incubators count as items too!

ITEMS

130/350

Potion

A spray-type medicine for treating wounds. It restores the HP of one Pokémon by 20 points.

x48

Revive

A medicine that can revive fainted Pokémon. It also restores half of a fainted Pokémon's maximum HP.

x30

Incense

Incense with a mysterious fragrance that lures wild Pokémon to your location for 30 minutes.

x4

Poké Ball

A device for catching wild Pokémon. It's thrown like a ball at a Pokémon, comfortably encaps... its target.

x38

Lure Module

POTIONS AND REVIVES

Once you get to Level 5 and start battling in Gyms, you will need those Potions and Revives you have been stockpiling. As you battle, you are going to have Pokémon get injured and even knocked out. In order to get those Pokémon battling again, you need Potions and Revives.

To heal an injured Pokémon and get more HP back, you need to use Potions. Here is a Potion List, what level you can obtain them, and what they do:

Potion, Level 5: Restores 20 HP to an injured Pokémon

Super Potion, Level 10: Restores 50 HP to an injured Pokémon

Hyper Potion, Level 15: Restores 200 HP to an injured Pokémon

Max Potion, Level 25: Restores an injured Pokémon to full HP

Whenever Pokémon are knocked out, you will need to use a Revive to get those Pokémon back on their feet. When used, it will not only revive them but will give them back half of their HP. At Level 30 you can obtain Max Revives, which revive your Pokémon and bring them back to full HP!

Most Pokémon will be healed with one Hyper Potion; if they have a lot more than average HP, such as Chansey or Snorlax, it might take two or three. By the time you get to Hyper Potions, you will find that regular Potions don't do enough and you will likely just trash them to keep your bag clear for other items. If you know you are going to do a lot of Gym battles, make sure you are well stocked on Potions first. You might have to heal as many as six Pokémon after a battle!

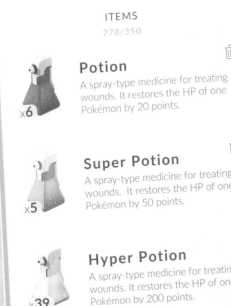

ITEMS
278/350

Potion
A spray-type medicine for treating wounds. It restores the HP of one Pokémon by 20 points.
x6

Super Potion
A spray-type medicine for treating wounds. It restores the HP of one Pokémon by 50 points.
x5

Hyper Potion
A spray-type medicine for treating wounds. It restores the HP of one Pokémon by 200 points.
x39

Revive
A medicine that can revive fainted Pokémon. It also restores half of a fainted Pokémon's maximum HP.
x37

Lucky Egg

INCENSE AND LURE MODULES

You can always go out walking to find Pokémon, but sometimes it's nice to have the Pokémon come to you.

That is where Incense and Lure Modules come in handy. Both items will last for 30 minutes. Both of these items will cause the Pokémon to be more attracted to you, but both do so in different ways. It's important to understand the differences.

The Incense will cause Pokémon to be attracted to you, no matter where you are. You are surrounded by a pink gassy circle which shows the Incense is working. At least once every five minutes, you should see a Pokémon in the area that has the pink circles around it too. This Pokémon cannot be seen by other GO players in the area. Incense is useful if you're in a rural area and in the mood to catch some Pokémon. Incense will bring one Pokemon every 5 minutes.

Lure Modules, on the other hand, must be installed in a Pokéstop. Once initiated, pink petals will rain over the Pokéstop. Like Incense, Lure Modules bring

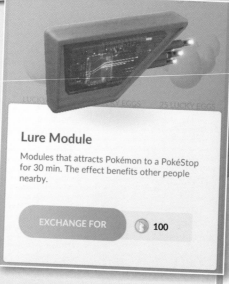

Lure Module

Modules that attracts Pokémon to a PokéStop for 30 min. The effect benefits other people nearby.

EXCHANGE FOR 100

Incense

Incense with a mysterious fragrance that lures wild Pokémon to your location for 30 minutes.

EXCHANGE FOR 80

Pokémon to you. Unlike Incense, the Pokémon that show up appear for all GO players in the area, making this great for a group of people. Make sure you stay near the Pokéstop, though—if you walk away, you won't see the extra Pokémon. A Lure will bring one Pokemon every 3 minutes.

Some places are particularly great for placing Lure Modules. One place is what we call "Pokéhubs." Pokéhubs are areas with many Pokéstops in a very small area. Pokéhubs can draw hundreds of people at a time. These are great places to set your Lures and still walk around. Many times when you visit Pokéhubs, the folks may have already placed Lures in the stops before you get there.

Other great places for Lures are near restaurants and pubs. We know restaurant owners near Pokéstops who Lure up their businesses and even offer discounts to GO players to get them to come inside. There's an ice cream shop and a pizza place near us that do this.

Both Incense and Lure Modules are fantastic for farming Pokémon when you want a bunch of Candy or Stardust, too!

RAZZ BERRIES

As you level up, you are going to find Pokémon with higher and higher CP, which means they will be harder and harder to catch. Eventually you will find Pokémon that are very hard to catch even with Great Balls and Ultra Balls. When that happens, you are going to need a little something extra—after all, you don't want that legendary Pokémon to appear and then have it run away.

When you need that something extra, reach into your bag and pull out a Razz Berry. A Razz Berry will make a Pokémon about one level easier to catch.

Razz Berries can turn a Pokémon's yellow capture circles into green circles, and red circles into orange circles. You don't even have to be stingy with Berries—you will usually find more Razz Berries than you need from Pokéstops.

Once used, Razz Berries will work for one successful throw. If the Pokémon breaks free from the Pokéball, you will need to use another Razz Berry to affect the next throw. If you miss the Pokémon completely with your toss, though, the Razz Berry is still working. The game will not let you use a Razz Berry unless it is useful to you, so don't worry about accidentally using one when you don't need to.

You will receive some Razz Berries as a reward for reaching Level 8. Razz Berries will start appearing at Pokéstops when you reach Level 8 as well.

Since you can get a lot of Razz Berries free from Pokéstops, don't be afraid to use them on what you desire most. If you crave a Charizard, use them every time you see a Charmander! If you want a Raichu, use a Razz Berry every time you see a Pikachu.

LUCKY EGGS

Lucky Eggs are a great way to level up faster because they double the XP (experience) you gain for 30 minutes.

You will get free Lucky Eggs when you reach Levels 9, 10, 15, 20, 25, 30, 35, and 40. You can also buy Lucky Eggs at the Shop.

When you are first starting out, we recommend using a few Lucky Eggs to gain a lot of XP quickly. This can rapidly get you to better Pokémon and get you a lot of supplies. As you continue to level up, however, you will find that the amount of XP you gain from a Lucky Egg in relation to the amount you need to level starts to get really bad, especially once some Pokémon start breaking out of their balls multiple times.

There is a still a really good trick to using Lucky Eggs to get thousands and thousands of extra XP. It's something we obviously call the "Lucky Egg Trick."

When you catch Pokémon and transfer Pokémon to Professor Willow, you will get a lot of Candy. You are going to want to stockpile as much Candy as you can until you can evolve about 60 Pokémon at one time. The best Pokémon for this are Pidgey, Weedle, and Caterpie, who only need 12 Candy to evolve. But you can include any other Pokémon that are ready to evolve in the trick as well. Once you've built up your resources, use a Lucky Egg and then evolve your Pokémon as fast as you can. We have found that you can evolve about 60

Since you get 500 XP per Pokémon Pokémon in 30 minutes gives you best value from your Lucky Eggs.

If you aren't all that great at math Lucky Eggs, well then you're in luck! programs that can help you out. For how many Pidgeys you should keep, transfer to Professor Willow for Egg, try an app like "Lucky Egg for PidgeyCalc.com. Just google "Pidgey plenty of assistance!

ITEM MANAGEMENT TIPS

When you start playing Pokémon GO, you will have 350 spaces in your bag. After excluding the Camera and the infinite-use Egg Incubator, that leaves 348. If you manage your items correctly, you should never have to purchase additional bag space.

Here is a great set of guidelines on how to best manage your items:

- First, keep an eye on your inventory count. Once you get in the 300 range, you should begin taking action. Since you can receive up to eight items from a Pokéstop, you can reach the 350 maximum pretty quickly. If you reach 350 Items, going to a Pokéstop will give you nothing. Since you want as many Pokéballs as possible, that's not a good thing. You should look over your items at this point and get rid of the nonessentials.

- Unless you plan on spending time at a Gym, you are likely to have more Revives than you need. You should get this down to 15 or 20 total.

- Potions are next. We would take it down to 25 or 30 of your best Potion, or use your top two potions if you don't have 25 or 30 of the best one.

- Lastly, Razz Berries can be very plentiful. A good guide is to keep the same number of Razz Berries as your level, up to Level 19. Once you hit Level 20, keep about 1½ times of your current level, because breakouts are very common there. Some people like to hoard Razz Berries for rare Pokémon.

If you aren't battling at Gyms, and don't plan to do so for a while, you can temporarily ditch all of your Potions and Revives. You can easily get more at future Pokéstops when you're ready to hit the Gyms!

After following these simple rules, you should have plenty of room for Pokéballs! And you'll be ready for some long hunts!

SHINE SHOP

The Shop will let you buy supplies using Pokécoins, Pokémon GO's in-game currency. You can earn Pokécoins by defending Gyms, or by spending real money. (We discuss defending Gyms later in our guide.)

So what can you buy with Pokécoins?

- You can buy Pokéballs, but we don't recommend buying them. You can load up on Pokéballs just by going to Pokéstops. We would only buy Pokéballs if we were truly desperate and an extremely rare Pokémon was around.

- You can buy a single Incense, or buy in bulk. We don't recommend buying any Incense unless you live in a very rural area and don't mind paying money to play this game.

- You can buy Lucky Eggs, which are priced the same as the Incense. We don't really recommend buying Lucky Eggs. Just use the free ones you get as you level.

- Lure Modules come in singles or an 8-pack. We wouldn't recommend buying Lure Modules unless you are a real-world store owner and have the capability to lure players to your store. Or you may want to buy them if you are meeting a group of friends at a Pokéstop to hang out.

- Egg Incubators can only be purchased for 150 coins each. We have found these to be the things we spend our coins on the most because they help you progress. They can help you find strong and rare Pokémon more quickly.

- The Shop will also allow you to upgrade your bag (to hold more items), and your Pokémon storage (to hold more Pokémon). You should be able to manage without having to buy these, but they aren't bad purchases, especially if you go on longer hunts.

- Lastly, you can purchase coins with your real money. The values get better the more you buy in bulk, with the highest being about a 30% discount over the smallest. 100 coins will cost about $1 U.S., meaning coins cost about 1 cent each. If you buy in bulk, you can get that price down to about 7/10th's of a penny per coin.

Remember, you do not have to spend a single penny on this game to enjoy it. Please only buy items if you can afford to do so. If we play "freemium" games for a while, we usually give the creators a few dollars for giving us the enjoyment.

Pojo Note: Android users might want to consider joining "Google Opinion Rewards" to get money to play Pokémon GO. Google will pay you with "Google Play Credits" to take various surveys, which in turn you can use to make purchases on anything from the Google Play Store. My friends and I have all made about $100 each taking these surveys. That buys a lot of Incubators!

THE POKÉMON CAMERA

The Camera is one of the cooler items that you have in your bag, and the resulting photos you get are different from just capturing screenshots. If you've been on social media, you've seen some great Pokémon GO pictures. People have put Pokémon into real-life situations and done it flawlessly and fluidly.

To do this, make sure that the AR (Augmented Reality) toggle button is turned "on" to see the Pokémon in the real world around you. The switch is in the upper-right corner of your screen when you are in the "Capture Pokémon" screen.

Make sure you are pointed in the direction of the Pokémon, because you won't be able to move the Pokémon around. In the bottom right, hit the Camera button, which will bring up a traditional camera screen with the shutter button at the bottom. Once you have everything lined up the way you want, you can take the picture.

If you like the image, hit the checkmark to save it. If you don't like it, hit the trash can. If you checkmark it, it will save the image to your phone's picture gallery, just like any other photo. You don't have to panic; the Pokémon will stick around for a while.

The Camera will clean up the picture by removing on-screen game buttons. It also puts your Trainer name at the bottom right of the picture, which is really cool because then anyone you show it to will know that you took it.

The only times you'd want to do a screenshot instead of using the Camera is if you want the Pokémon's name and their CP displayed in the picture, or if you want to show your friends a screenshot of a cool location you've found on the Map Screen.

SETTINGS SCREEN

The Settings Screen is where you can change some of the settings for Pokémon GO.

If you'd rather play with the music off, you can. Some people like listening to their own music on headphones while playing, which the game lets you do.

Next you can turn off sound effects, and the button after that is vibration. We don't recommend turning either of these off. Both are great clues for when you're near a Pokéstop, leave a Pokéstop, or find a Pokémon.

Next is the battery saver mode. Pokémon GO can be a battery hog on long walks. Switch on battery saver and your phone will go automatically dim when it's down by your side in a horizontal position. But alerts continue to operate. You will be notified of Pokémon and Pokéstops, and your steps will still count towards Egg hatching. This is a fantastic setting to save battery life and doesn't affect the quality of your experience. You also might want to go into your phone's menu and disable any auto-lock setting that turns your screen off after a certain amount of time, just to make sure you're not missing any Pokémon.

Another nice feature is the ability to change your nickname one time.

You can also go to the help center, report a high-priority issue, see which version of the game you have, and sign out of the game.

Signing out of the game can come in handy if you have two accounts. Some people have a Google account as well as a completely different Trainer's Club account. If you love playing Pokémon GO, and the Trainer's Club is down, maybe the Google account will let you in to keep playing. You won't share Pokémon between accounts, but you're still having fun catching 'em all!

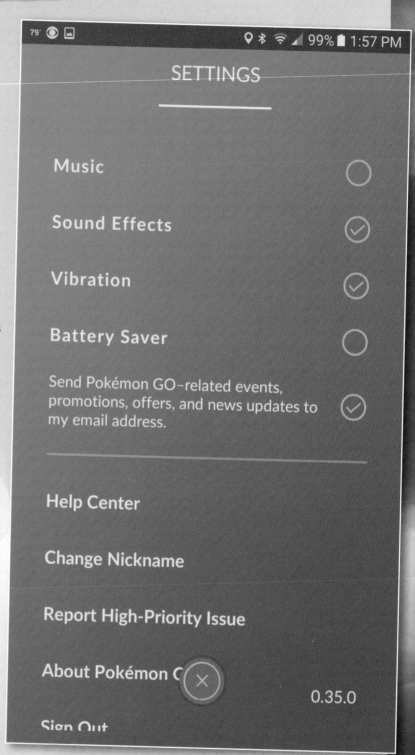

TRANSFERRING POKÉMON TO PROFESSOR WILLOW

As you go on Pokémon expeditions, you are going to catch a lot of Pokémon.

A lot of those Pokémon will be duplicates of ones you have already captured, and some will have really low IVs (discussed later in the book). Those low-IV Pokémon are not worth leveling up, so your best option is to transfer them to Professor Willow to free up space for more valuable Pokémon.

In return for the transfer, the Professor will give you back one Candy of that Pokémon type. While it's not a lot, it certainly adds up over time and is very important for both evolving and leveling up your Pokémon.

Some people will see the same Pokémon over and over and think, "I don't need to catch this—I have already caught a lot these." Not true at all! Those Pokémon you capture are going to give you a little XP when you capture them, and a ton of Candy over time—which will let you evolve a whole bunch more Pokémon and get a ton of XP.

To evolve a Magikarp into Gyarados, you need 400 Candies! You're going to need to catch 101 boring Magikarp in total if you want a Gyarados. (Catching a Magikarp gives three Candies and transferring to Professor Willow another one.)

We're not even sad to see a Pidgey, because we know each one is almost like getting about 125 bonus XP once we evolve them! So make sure you collect a bunch of the Candy—it's one of the biggest keys to becoming a high-level Pokémon Trainer!

Pojo's Note: The transfer button can be reached through the menu button at the bottom right of each individual Pokémon's screen.

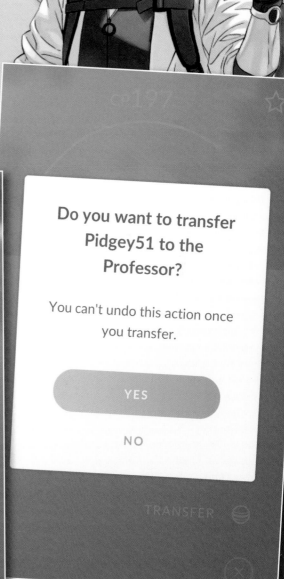

WHAT ARE POKÉMON GO IVs?

"IVs" stands for Individual Values. Every Pokémon you catch is unique. Each Pokémon essentially has different genes than every other Pokémon you've caught. In the real world, Bill and Butch might both be six feet tall and weigh 200 pounds, but Bill might be faster than Butch, while Butch might be stronger than Bill. Pokémon are no different!

Your Pokémon's CP (Combat Power) indicates how well that particular Pokémon will perform in battle. Not all Pokémon have the same CP—for example, if you have caught two Bulbasaur, they will not necessarily have the same CP. It is a safe assumption that Pokémon with higher CPs will generally do better in Gym battles. But it is not a safe assumption that a Pokémon with a higher CP will always be stronger than a Pokémon with lower CP. Even two Pokémon with the same CP might not be equal. Once fully powered up and fully evolved, a lower CP Pokémon might actually be much stronger in the end. So do not just simply toss lower CP Pokémon aside because you have a higher CP Pokémon in your Pokédex. We need to find out your Pokémon's hidden stats!

Every Pokémon you catch in Pokémon GO has three hidden stats which make up their Individual Values. These hidden stats are Attack, Defense, and Stamina. All species of Pokémon have base statistics for Attack, Defense, and Stamina. Some Pokémon will have their base statistics plus a little extra bonus. That little extra bonus will be a random number from 0-15 to each of their three hidden stats.

As an example, let's say we catch three Scythers. One is the worst possible, one is average, and one is the best possible. All Scythers' base stats are 176 Attack, 180 Defense, and 140 Stamina.

> The worst Scyther would be getting Base Statistics + no bonus for Attack, Defense, or Stamina. Final Score = 176/180/140

> The average Scyther would be getting Base Statistics + about 1/2 bonus for Attack, Defense. or Stamina. Final Score = 183/187/147

> The best Scyther would be getting Base Statistics + max bonus for Attack, Defense, or Stamina. Final Score = 191/195/155

So if you have the worst possible Scyther, the average Scyther will be about 4.5% stronger, and the best Scyther will be about 9% better.

Many people want to try to obtain the "best of the best" species for their collection to give them advantages in Gym battles. The in-game "Appraise" feature and other IV calculators can give you clues to finding your best Pokémon.

CP85

Scyther

HP 23 / 23

Bug / Flying	50.95 kg	1.5 m
Type	Weight	Height

103613
STARDUST

3
SCYTHER CANDY

POWER UP   200   1

Steel Wing
Steel

Night Slash   30

After you catch Pokémon, you can see each Pokémon's CP (Combat Power). Combat Power is a simple statistic based on averaging out the Pokémon's hidden stats. You can also see the Pokémon's CP Arc (the semicircle over the Pokémon) and the Pokémon's Hit Points (HP). IV calculators can take this information and calculate your Pokémon IVs.

How to determine your strongest Pokémon

One way is to ask your Team Leader through the "Appraise" feature. We discuss this feature in the next section of the book. The only problem with this feature is your Team Leader only gives you a range of values through vague answers. Your leader will not tell you the exact IV of your Pokémon.

The other way is you use an IV calculator. These are not built into the game but you can find them online. An IV calculator will calculate your Pokémon's hidden values for you and make it easier to compare Pokémon at different CP levels. This will help you determine which Pokémon to keep and power up and evolve, and which Pokémon to transfer to Professor Willow.

How to use an IV calculator

One of the easiest calculators for new players to use is the IV Rater from Silph Road.

- Select your Pokémon's Species

- Enter your existing trainer level

- Slide the CP Arc to match your Pokémon's arc. (This can be a little tough to eyeball. Tip: all Pokémon you catch in the wild are "whole #'s, with no decimal points" if you haven't powered them up at all)

- Enter your Pokémon's CP

- Enter your Pokémon's HP

- Hit "Rate my Pokémon"

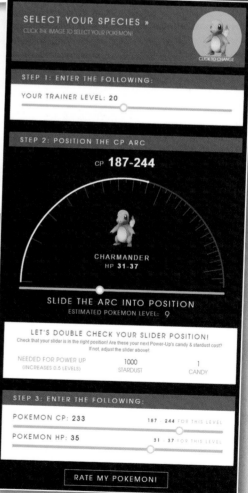

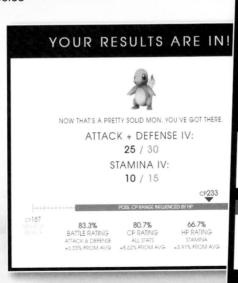

This book is not sponsored, endorsed by, or otherwise affiliated with any companies or the products featured in the book. This is not an official publication.

39

The Silph Road IV Rater will give you one of five results, from bad to great:

- Oh dear. You may want to send this one to the Professor. Afraid it's not gonna be competitive, traveler. :/

- This mon's IVs are a little worse than 'middle of the road' it seems, traveler.

- Now that's a pretty solid mon, you've got there. Not perfect, but definitely a decent fighter!

- Now that's a pretty solid mon, you've got there.

- Wow, traveler. This mon has perfect IVs! Hang on to this one!

These results make it easy to determine which Pokémon you want to keep. We transfer our Pokémon to Professor Willow if we get the first two (bad) results, and maybe even if we get average results. We generally keep the rest until it comes to evolution time. We give the keepers the "Favorite" star as soon as we make the decision to keep them. This way you know you've already reviewed them, plus you can't accidentally transfer them to Professor Willow.

The percentages at the bottom show how close your Pokémon is to Perfect IVs (15/15/15). The middle number is the most important—50% is average, 100% is perfect. We find it helpful to rename your Pokémon after you calculate their rating if you decide to keep them. If your Eevee gets a CP Rating of 71, rename it "Eevee71". That will help you ultimately decide who to dismiss, keep, and evolve. And by renaming them, you know you have already run the stats on them, and won't have to do it again. Results will be more accurate as the Pokémon's CP gets higher and higher..

Let's look at that Charmander again. "Candela told us that Charmander is a Strong Pokémon. You should be proud!" How proud should we be? Well, the IV Rater says our Charmander has a CP rating of 80.7%. This includes all stats (Attack, Defense, and Stamina). His Battle Rating is 83.3%—this excludes his stamina. And his HP rating is 66.7%. We're going to rename him Charmander80 and keep farming Charmander Candy. We'll keep looking for a better Charmander, but if we don't find one, we'll evolve this guy. He's a pretty solid mon, and we're proud!

Is there such a thing as a perfect Pokémon? Do any Pokémon have perfects IV's?

Yes, but they can be pretty rare to find. But you may find a couple by the time you reach Level 20. Make sure you raise those Pokémon to their utmost capabilities, and pray you get some good attacks along with those stats. The Goldeen in the next section has perfect IVs.

Are there other IV calculators or apps?

Yes, there are other IV calculators online that you can use. Many are very good. Find one you like and get comfortable with it.

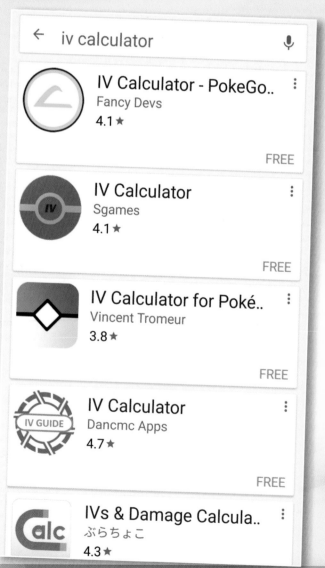

There are also some fantastic apps you can download from Google Play or the iTunes store. There are also great videos on YouTube explaining how to use IV calculators if you are still confused.

Important IV notes

The IV strength of a Pokémon will stay with it as you evolve it. A 92% Squirtle will become a 92% Wartortle, and then a 92% Blastoise! IVs will not change, but Movesets do change when you evolve.

Pokémon hatched from Eggs are usually higher level Pokémon. We usually give them the Favorite star as soon as they hatch, so that we don't accidentally transfer them. Don't be too mad when you get a Pokémon from an Egg you already have in your Pokédex. Generally, it will be a really strong Pokémon, and give you a lot of Candy.

One thing we've noticed when hunting with groups of friends is that if we all caught the same Pokémon, that Pokémon will have the same IVs for everyone. It might have different CP, but the IVs will come out to be the same in an IV calculator. We even noticed that the Pokémon had the same height, weight, and Movesets for all of us as well. Compare with your friends!

Does all this work really make a difference?

A little. Not much, but a little. All Pokémon are guaranteed to at least have their base statistics. If you have the worst possible Pokémon stat-wise, you still have the minimum baseline statistics. The average equal Pokémon would be about 5% stronger, and the absolute perfect Pokémon would be about 10% stronger. Usually, a Pokémon's attacks are much more important than their base statistics.

If you are a person who needs the absolute best Pokémon, use an IV calculator to try and get them. If you really don't care, just take the highest CP Pokémon you have and max it out. It'll probably only mean 5% difference on average anyway, and will save you some Candy.

To summarize, we recommend checking IVs if you are farming difficult Pokémon to evolve such as Charmander, Bulbasaur, Squirtle, Dragonair, Magikarp, etc. You might as well evolve the very best since you've worked hard finding them!

CP 1073

Blastoise

HP 93 / 93

| Water | 98.52 kg | 1.75 m |
| Type | Weight | Height |

| 1426 | 72 |
| STARDUST | SQUIRTLE CANDY |

POWER UP | 1900 | 2

Water Gun
Water

Ice Beam

65

THE APPRAISAL FEATURE

You chose a team when you turned Level 5. Each team has a Leader:

Team Mystic (Blue)—Blanche

Team Valor (Red)—Candela

Team Instinct (Yellow)—Spark

In late August 2016, a new feature was added to Pokémon GO called "Appraise." This new feature allows players to ask their Leaders about the power level of any Pokémon they own. Basically, this lets you quickly check a range of IVs of your Pokémon without leaving the game. This is Niantic's answer to IV checkers people are using outside of the game. The Appraise feature is simple, it works, and we like it.

The hard part at first is determining what the phrases actually mean, and each Leader has a different way of telling you what IV range your Pokémon is in. They will discuss the Pokémon's overall strength, its defense and/or attack, and the Pokémon's size. We think the first critique they give is the most important, and that's the Overall Power of the Pokémon.

On the next page are the key phrases in determining the Overall Power of your Pokémon.

How should you use these results?

You can use this Appraisal feature every time you catch a Pokémon. If the Pokémon's IVs are below 50% you should probably transfer them to Professor Willow, unless they are very rare Pokémon with a high CP. You should probably keep the highest-CP Pokémon you have for all Stage 2 Pokémon and extremely rare Pokémon until you get stronger replacements. If you're Appraising common and uncommon Pokémon, though, you can safely transfer any Pokémon that falls into the bottom two categories.

We think if you get the Top 2 results you should probably keep the Pokémon until it's time to evolve or power them up. Then you might want to use an external IV rater to get more specific results, such as the ones we discussed earlier in the book. Then you can pick your very best Pokémon to evolve or power up.

In the end, you need to be the judge on what Pokémon you want to keep. If you want a Golduck just for attacking Gyms, you might want to keep a Golduck or Psyduck with a high Attack Feature, even if its overall Power is mediocre.

After you have Appraised a Pokémon and have decided to keep it, you might want to rename it, just so you know the Appraising has been done. We graded an Eevee in the images, and Candela gave it her 2nd best review. So we could name it "Eevee2."

Mystic (Blanche)—Blue	IV Range
Overall, your Pokémon is a wonder! What a breathtaking Pokémon!	81% to 100%
Overall, your Pokémon has certainly caught my attention.	67% to 80%
Overall, your Pokémon is above average.	51% to 66%
Overall, your Pokémon is not likely to make much headway in battle.	0% to 50%

Valor (Candela)—Red	IV Range
Overall, your Pokémon simply amazes me. It can accomplish anything!	81% to 100%
Overall, your Pokémon is a strong Pokémon. You should be proud!	67% to 80%
Overall, your Pokémon is a decent Pokémon.	51% to 66%
Overall, your Pokémon may not be great in battle, but I still like it!	0% to 50%

Instinct (Spark)—Yellow	IV Range
Overall, your Pokémon looks like it can really battle with the best of them!	81% to 100%
Overall, your Pokémon is really strong!	67% to 81%
Overall, your Pokémon is pretty decent!	51% to 66%
Overall, your Pokémon has room for improvement as far as battling goes.	0% to 50%

LEVELING UP AND POWERING UP

Now that you know how to figure out who your strongest IV Pokémon are, you are going to want power them up. But this requires both Stardust and Candy.

As your Pokémon's Combat Power gets higher, the amount of Stardust and Candy necessary to power them up goes up as well. As tempting as it might be, we would strongly advise all Pokémon Trainers not to power up any Pokémon until you reach Level 15—and that's only if you plan on doing Gym battles. Otherwise, hold off until you've reached Level 20.

Up until Level 20, you will gain levels pretty quickly, simply by catching Pokémon. We recommend that you keep grinding away, earning XP by catching Pokémon, spinning Pokéstops, and doing the Lucky Egg Trick a few times.

Once you hit Level 20, however, it becomes a lot harder to level up further. So if you use all your Candy and Stardust on a Pokémon early, you could very easily find a Pokémon in the wild shortly after with even better IV—with no Stardust or Candy available. If you are a patient Trainer, you can have an absolutely huge Pokémon army just from catching wild Pokémon. Now is a good time to start powering up and evolving strong IV Pokémon.

You are limited on how high you can train a Pokémon based on your level. There is a dot on the Pokémon's CP Arc (the semi-circle behind your Pokémon). The closer it gets to the bottom right, the closer you are to its maximum training for that level. Once you level up as a Trainer, you can go back and make the Pokémon bigger, too.

Just remember that patience is a virtue, and if you're going to spend Candy and Stardust, you want that Pokémon to be good for a long time.

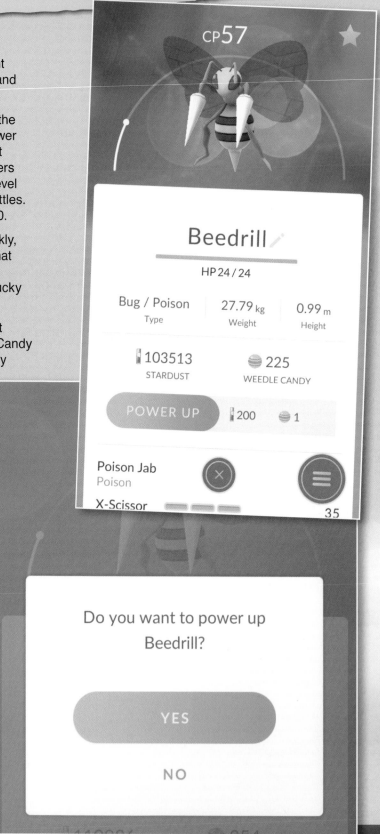

EVOLVING HIGH-LEVEL POKÉMON

Okay, we taught you how to find your best IV Pokémon, and you've patiently waited until Level 20. Now you're ready to start evolving Pokémon! Evolving Pokémon works a bit different from powering up Pokémon, so read on!

- No Stardust is consumed by evolving, only a lot of that Pokémon's Candy.

- You will gain XP from evolving. Evolving a Pokémon gives you 500 XP, and if it's new to your Pokédex, you will get 1,000 XP. Evolving can certainly be a great way to get a lot of XP fast and start shooting up levels.

- Evolving a Pokémon might change its "Moveset" (its Regular and Special Attacks). Usually, but not always, the evolved Pokémon will learn some different moves.

Earlier in the book we told you about the Lucky Egg Trick. The Lucky Egg Trick is great for evolving common Pokémon like Pidgey, Weedle, Rattata, and Caterpie.

Now we're going to discuss the evolving of the high-level Pokémon you crave, like Charizard, Blastoise, Venusaur, Dragonite, etc. We think you should wait until you have 125 Candies before evolving them, so you can go straight to their Stage 2 level.

Why? We think it gives you the best bang for your buck. Let's say you want to make everyone's favorite Pokemon, Charizard. To make a Charizard, you need to catch 32 wild Charmanders to get 125 Candies. (This will be less if you happen to hatch one.) You can evolve a Charmander to Charmeleon when you have 25 Candies, but during the time it takes you to get 100 more Candies, you might find a better IV Charmander!

Our recommendation:

- Keep catching wild basic Pokémon

- Run IVs and only keep your best 1-3 basic Pokémon

- Transfer the least-desirable Pokémon to Professor Willow

- Collect 125 Candies

- Pick the very best IV Pokémon to evolve

- Evolve it straight from Base to Stage 1, and directly to Stage 2

- Power up your Pokémon to the fullest (unless you don't like their Moveset)

While waiting for 125 Candies, you might even find a Stage 1 Pokémon that has better IVs than the base set Pokémon you've been collecting. This will save you 25 Candy!

This recommendation is perfect for all Stage 2 Pokémon. For something like Eevee, though, it's a bit different. You might want to keep your best 3-5 IV Eevees around to evolve. Eevee-lutions are very strong in Pokémon GO. It only costs 25 Eevee Candy to evolve them. Keep evolving them until you get their most desirable Movesets (we'll cover that later in the book).

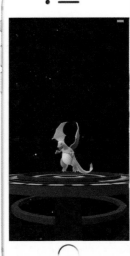

Now let's check our CP 77 Bulbasaur: Holy cow! He gets a CP score of 88.2%. That means that once fully evolved, he will be about 88% better than the Base Statistics. That's excellent! This lower-CP Bulbasaur will turn out to be about 6% stronger Venusaur than our 305 CP Bulbasaur once fully evolved. We would be fine evolving this Bulbasaur into Venusaur if we didn't find a better one once we had 125 Candies.

Moral of the story: don't be fooled by CP alone! Ask your Team Leader to Appraise your Pokémon, and/or run your Pokémon through an IV checker if you want the very best Pokémon! Remember, the IV percentages will stay with each Pokémon all the way through to their final evolution.

We thought we'd give you an example of possibly being duped by a high-level CP Pokémon, versus a low-level CP Pokémon.

When everyone first starts playing Pokémon GO, they look straight at a Pokémon's CP (Combat Points). They keep the highest CP Pokémon, and transfer the lower ones to Professor Willow for Candy. We admit, we did that for a few weeks, too, until a bunch of people smarter than us figured out you could find each Pokémon's hidden stats through an Individual Values (IV) checker.

Here are two of our Bulbasaurs. One's CP = 305. The other's CP = 77.

But before we transfer the lower-CP one to Professor Willow, let's compare their IVs. (We're using the online "IV Rater" from TheSilphRoad.com for this example, but you can also use the Appraiser feature inside Pokémon GO.)

First, let's check the IV of our CP 305 Bulbasaur: Wow! His projected stats are all below average. That means that once fully evolved, he will be about 22.5% better than the Base Statistics (50% would be average). This isn't that good. You should probably be shooting for 80% or higher on something that takes so much Candy to evolve.

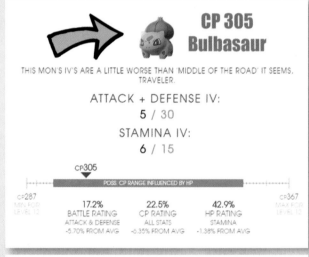

CP 305 Bulbasaur

THIS MON'S IV'S ARE A LITTLE WORSE THAN 'MIDDLE OF THE ROAD' IT SEEMS, TRAVELER.

ATTACK + DEFENSE IV:
5 / 30

STAMINA IV:
6 / 15

CP305

POSS. CP RANGE INFLUENCED BY HP

| CP287 MIN FOR LEVEL 13 | 17.2% BATTLE RATING ATTACK & DEFENSE -5.70% FROM AVG | 22.5% CP RATING ALL STATS -0.35% FROM AVG | 42.9% HP RATING STAMINA -1.36% FROM AVG | CP367 MAX FOR LEVEL 13 |

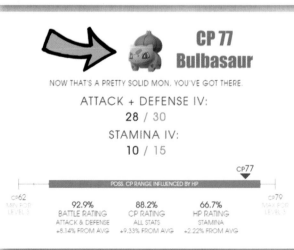

CP 77 Bulbasaur

NOW THAT'S A PRETTY SOLID MON. YOU'VE GOT THERE.

ATTACK + DEFENSE IV:
28 / 30

STAMINA IV:
10 / 15

CP77

POSS. CP RANGE INFLUENCED BY HP

| CP62 MIN FOR LEVEL 9 | 92.9% BATTLE RATING ATTACK & DEFENSE +8.14% FROM AVG | 88.2% CP RATING ALL STATS +9.33% FROM AVG | 66.7% HP RATING STAMINA +2.22% FROM AVG | CP79 MAX FOR LEVEL 9 |

POWERING UP AND EVOLVING: WHICH TO DO FIRST

Some of the most common questions we get involve evolving Pokémon. Here are some questions we get asked often:

- Should I power up a Pokémon first and then evolve it, or evolve a Pokémon and then power it up?

- Which method uses the least Candy and Stardust?

Let's tackle the second question first:

Which method uses the least Candy and Stardust? *It doesn't matter.* To fully evolve a Pokémon and power it up, you will ultimately spend the exact same amount of Stardust and Candy either way. The math works out the same.

When it comes to powering up first vs. evolving first, *we prefer evolving a Pokémon first.* Why? Because we want our Pokémon to have the very best Movesets, and we want to waste as little Candy and Stardust as possible in our attempts to get them. A Pokémon's Movesets will usually change when you evolve them.

Here's an example: let's say we're trying to evolve a Staryu into a Starmie with the best Moveset. This Staryu has 95% IVs, so it's a very good one. In the Pokédex we see that Starmie's top Moveset is:

- Water Gun / Swift

We know evolving a Staryu into a fully powered up Starmie will cost the same amount of Candy and Stardust either way we try it. And we really

want to see what Starmie's attacks are going to be first, so we evolve our best Staryu into Starmie without powering it up first. We don't want to waste any Staryu Candy or Stardust powering it up unnecessarily. So we spend 50 Staryu Candy and evolve it. And we get a Starmie with the Moveset:

- Tackle / Psychic

Darn it! That's not what we wanted. We didn't get either of the best secondary Attacks in the Pokedex, which are Quick Attack / Power Gem. It's back to the drawing board for us. We will keep this Starmie for now until we get one with better attacks, but we're not going to spend any Stardust or extra Candy powering it up. We saved a lot of Stardust and Candy by finding out early and not powering up Staryu first. We think you should do this any time you want a powerful Pokémon for Gym battles.

Pojo Note: *Notice in the images how the CP Arc over the Pokémon is in the exact same position after evolution. The Power Up Costs have not changed either. Also, your Pokémon's personal name stays with the Pokémon through the evolution as well.*

ATTACKING GYMS

We generally find that new players are intimidated by Gyms and Gym battles. The game doesn't go a great job of explaining Gyms, but we are here to help!

Gyms are special points of interest found throughout the world. You can capture a Gym for your team and battle the Pokémon of rival teams there. Gyms can be challenged by multiple Trainers at the same time.

A Gym's level is determined by its Prestige. As a Gym earns Prestige, it increases in level. The higher a Gym's level, the more Pokémon can be assigned to it, which makes it harder for rival teams to capture. A Gym's Prestige increases when you assign a trained Pokémon to it, and also when teammates assign additional Pokémon.

For every 2,000 points a Gym has, it gains one additional level. For every level, you can add an additional Pokémon from your team. One caveat—each Trainer can only have one Pokémon in a Gym. Other players from your team need to fill in the rest of the gym. Each Gym can hold between 1 and 10 Pokémon, depending on its Prestige.

Gyms on the GPS map can be one of four colors, each of which refers to the team that controls that Gym. Yellow, blue, and red represent Team Instinct, Team Mystic, and Team Valor, respectively. If the gym is white, that means nobody controls it, and the first team to put a Pokémon there will control it. To do that, tap on the Gym and there will be a button in the bottom left. Hit that button and then choose a Pokémon—it's that simple.

How you interact with Gyms, however, depends on whether or not you control it.

If your team does not control the Gym, then you can challenge it. Gym battles are fairly simple. You go into battle with a team of six Pokémon of your choosing. Once you have selected your Pokémon, you will then battle against the team that controls that Gym. You will attack their Pokémon in succession, from their weakest Pokémon to their strongest Pokémon. You can see all the Pokémon in the Gym by flicking the screen left or right with your finger before entering battle.

For every one of their Pokémon you knock out, their Gym will lose a little Prestige. If you knock all the Pokémon out, then their Gym will lose a *lot* of Prestige. If you knock the Gym down at least 2,000 points, it will kick out the weakest Pokémon. The next time you battle, you will need to defeat one fewer Pokémon, making the next battle even easier. This gives you a lot of XP as well, so it's not so bad when a rival controls a Gym. You can rinse and repeat until you have knocked out all of the Pokémon, and you will take over their Gym. Remember to revive and heal Pokémon after every battle!

After you defeat a Gym, it becomes vacant (white) and you can claim it for your own team. You simply put a Pokémon in the Gym as mentioned above. You will get 10 Pokécoins.

If your team does control the Gym, then you can train your Pokémon there. In this case, you select only one Pokémon and then battle as long you can against the Pokémon there. For each one you defeat, your Gym will gain a little Prestige and you gain a little XP. While the XP is better fighting against a rival Gym, if you can get a Pokémon into a Gym and keep it there for 20 hours, you get to collect free Pokécoins and Stardust, so you definitely want to put a strong Pokémon in the Gym. The higher the Gym's Prestige, the higher the level, and the more Pokémon that can be in the Gym. Always remember to check the Shop and see if free coins are waiting for you if you are a Gym battler.

The trick to battling your own Gyms is to take a Pokémon with lower CP, but a "Type Advantage" (explained below), because you will get more Prestige and more XP. Every 2,000 points will allow your team to add another defender to the Gym.

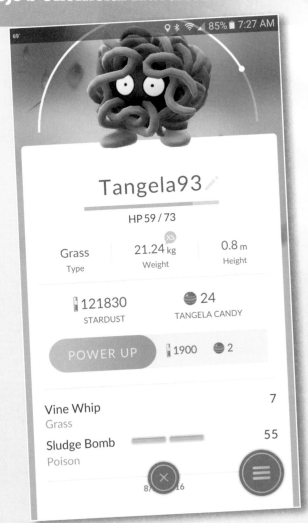

Special Attack. Keep in mind that doing so will use up the energy in that bar, and you need to refill it again using your Basic Attack.

Dodging

Your opponent's Pokémon is automatically attacking you as well, so you are going to want to avoid getting hit if you can, especially from Special Attacks. To do this, swipe quickly left or right on the screen with your finger. This will cause your Pokémon to move left or right to dodge an attack.

All defending Pokémon have different animations of their attacks. These animations are not that important for dodging, as they take different times for different defending Pokémon. But animations do indicate it's almost time to dodge. What is important is the "Flash" and "Lines" around the edge of the screen (see image). When you see those, it's time to swipe and dodge.

Battling and Movesets

Actual battling involves learning how to use your Pokémon's moves. Each Pokémon in Pokémon GO has two moves—a Basic Attack and a Special Attack. This is usually called its "Moveset." Your Pokémon's Moveset can be found on its individual Pokémon screen. We posted an image of our Tangela's Moveset. You can see it has two attacks—Vine Whip and Sludge Bomb. Vine Whip is its Basic Attack, while Sludge Bomb is its Special Attack.

To use the Pokémon's basic move, just tap anywhere on the screen. It really doesn't matter where you tap, though we prefer near the middle so we don't accidentally hit another button. As you do your Basic Attack, you will be building up your Special Attack. Once one of the blue bars under your name is full, you can use your Pokémon's Special Attack by pressing and holding on the screen for one second. The battle screen will show your Pokémon using its

Defending Pokémon attack you every two seconds. You will usually get in about 1-3 Basic Attacks depending on your Pokémon's Basic Attack animation speed (which varies for each Pokémon), and then you should prepare to dodge. Also, a defending Pokémon always seems to attack twice in a row when it first starts battling you. So be prepared to dodge twice at the very beginning of every Pokémon battle before you start attacking. Practice enough and you can avoid a lot of your opponent's attacks, and you'll get into a great rhythm of attacking and dodging.

Switching

During battles you can see two buttons at the bottom right of the screen. The Man Running Button will let you flee from battle. The Double Arrow Button will let you change your Pokémon during battle. If you see you are at a "Type Disadvantage" (explained in the next column), you can quickly change to one of your other Pokémon.

The Wolf Pack Attack!

Gym battles occur in real time—everyone on the same team who is attacking a Pokémon in a Gym at the same time will all damage the defending Pokémon concurrently. This is where you can use teamwork to take down even the biggest of Gyms. Before fighting, everyone should prepare their teams, and initiate the battle at about the same time. If you time it right, all of you can enter the Gym fight at the same time, and you can Wolf Pack Attack the Pokémon in there. While some high-level Gyms may be hard to attack alone, using two, three, or even more people to attack the defending Pokémon at once will make a huge difference in your total damage and how fast they get knocked out. It's also a great way for all of you to earn a ton of XP quickly!

Type Advantage

Another thing that can make a huge difference in winning Gym battles is matchups.

Your Pokémon can be weak or strong versus the Gym defender's Pokémon based on their Type. Fire is weak to Water. Grass is weak to Fire. There are 18 different Types in Pokémon, and all have strengths and weaknesses.

You want to try to maximize your advantage in these matchups when setting up your attacking team. You can see what Pokémon are in the Gym before entering battle, so prepare your team accordingly. A Pokémon's Type determines which attacks will have a Type Advantage against it. Later in the book is a Combat Chart that shows you the best attacks to use against other Pokémon.

Remember that each Pokémon, even those with the same name, can have a number of different attacks that could be of different types. The attack type determines Type Advantage over other Pokémon, not the attacking Pokémon's Type. Of course, your opponent will also be attacking you! Keep this in mind when choosing your Pokémon for battle.

Getting good matchups will allow you to take down defending Pokémon, even if they have a lot more CP than you. Take some time to study and soon you'll be controlling your own Gym!

SUPPORTING LOCAL BUSINESSES

As you are exploring and playing Pokémon GO, you will see that lot of Pokéstops and Gyms are actually inside or around businesses (retail stores, restaurants, ice cream parlors, pizza parlors, etc.).

Now, if you are just passing by outside and want to collect from that Pokéstop, that should be completely fine. If you are going to sit down because there is a Lure Module there, however, you should be respectful of that business.

This especially goes for restaurants. If a restaurant has enough people come in and not order anything, they will likely refuse to let Pokémon players inside anymore. You are using their facilities, so you need to do your part to support them. If you want to sit there, consider getting a meal or an appetizer, or at least a drink. That makes you a paying customer and will make the business happier to support Pokémon players.

We have even seen businesses who will give bonus discounts for Pokémon players, so you can take advantage of that while you are there. We're not saying you have to spend a lot of money every time you go, but you should support a business that is supporting you. If they weren't there, their business wouldn't have a Pokéstop and you wouldn't have a place to collect supplies and put Lure Modules. This is a great way of saying thank you to them.

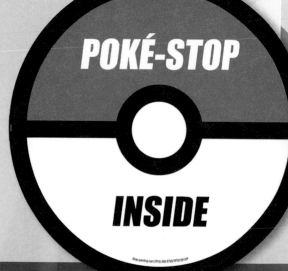

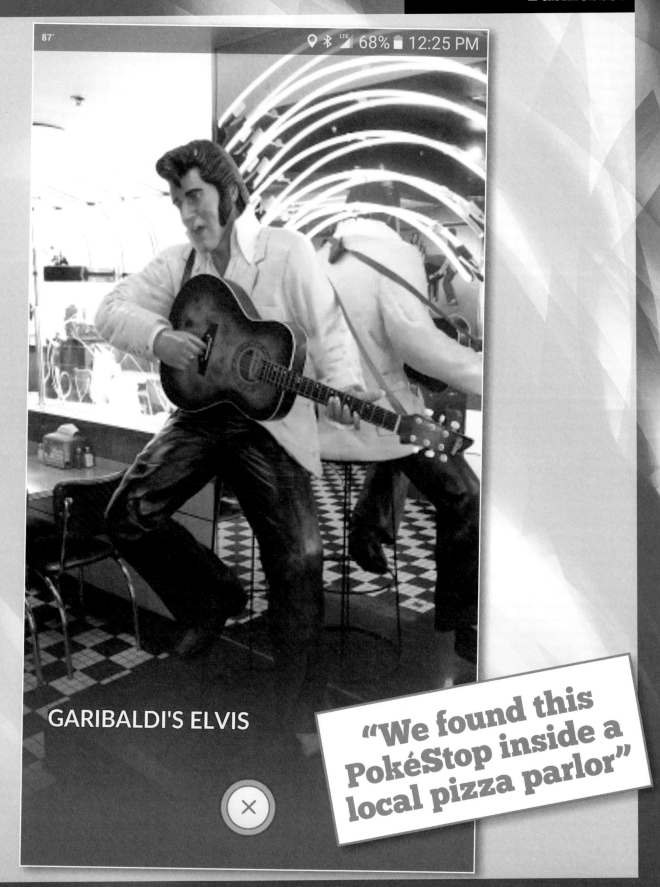

GARIBALDI'S ELVIS

"We found this PokéStop inside a local pizza parlor"

SOCIALIZING

One of the best aspects of Pokémon GO is the opportunity to be around a lot of other people while you're out playing the game. That is very different from most video games, where you usually are playing by yourself inside.

While you can certainly try to do everything on your own, you will find that talking to, and making friends with, other people will help a lot in your Pokémon GO journey.

Sometimes you will come across some rare and hard-to-find Pokémon on your Sightings Screen. When you do, you can ask other GO players if they have seen it and know where it is. We have found people to be very nice in this respect, and it has led

us to catching Pokémon we might not have found. Plus, you never know when you might make a new friend out there, and Pokéhunting is always more fun when you do it with friends.

We have a nest site near our office that is in a public park with a large pond and a 1-mile walking path around it. The rare Pokémon can spawn anywhere in the park. If we capture a rare one, we usually tell anyone else walking past us (that appears to be playing GO) what we discovered. On future laps around the park, they will usually respond in kind.

Sometimes your better-half might not play Pokémon GO, but they enjoy walking and they will keep you company on your hunt.

Sometimes you can hunt down Pokémon as a team, and spread out across parks and fields to help narrow the search.

Sometimes you'll want a big group of friends to help you take down a Gym.

And it's always easier to take fun GO pictures if you can include your friends in them.

On the flip side, do your best not to be rude to people. Don't have your phone's volume turned all the way up without headphones. Don't run into people to go catch a Pokémon. And If you do, apologize quickly for it. Being kind and polite will get you a whole lot further than being rude.

TAKING FUN PICTURES

We discussed taking pictures with your Pokémon camera earlier, and this is one place where you can really get creative. When a Pokémon appears with your AR turned on, try to think of a funny or ironic way to take its picture.

Abra is in the sitting down position. We've seen photos of Abra sitting on bus seats, trains, and even in the bathroom. We've seen Grass Pokémon in front of lawnmowers; Squirtle standing on an airplane wing; Exeggcutes near frying pans; Krabby at a Crab bar; Rattatas in restaurants; and many more.

This is an area where your imagination can just run wild. Try to come up with the funniest pictures you can think of, and then share them with your friends or put them on social media so lots of people can enjoy them.

There are Twitter accounts that are nothing but funny Pokémon GO pictures. You can laugh at those, and maybe it will give you some inspiration.

Now, you certainly don't have to do this kind of thing, and if it's not something that appeals to you, then don't feel like you are obligated. But taking creative pictures is just another reason why Pokémon GO has taken the world by storm!

Valensiakol

Unphi

Fragli

EEVEE-LUTIONS!

In Pokémon Red and Blue, you could evolve your Eevee using Stones. A Fire Stone yielded Flareon, a Water Stone yielded Vaporeon, and a Thunder Stone yielded Jolteon.

During the first season of the Pokémon Anime (1998), Ash Ketchum encounters "The Battling Eevee Brothers." The brothers are named Sparky, Rainier, and Pyro.

- Sparky has an Electric Eevee Evolution—Jolteon
- Rainer has a Water Eevee Evolution—Vaporeon
- Pyro has a Fire Eevee Evolution—Flareon

They are pushing their younger brother Mikey to evolve his Eevee into something. Mikey ultimately decides to keep his Eevee as an ever-loveable little Eevee—and of course his little Eevee takes down Team Rocket and saves the day.

When you normally evolve an Eevee in Pokémon GO, you will randomly get a Jolteon, Vaporeon, or Flareon. There are no "Eevee-lution Stones" in Pokémon GO. However, people have found an Easter Egg in Pokémon GO: if you rename your Eevee after one of the Battling Eevee brothers' names, you can control your Eevee-lution!

If you want a particular Eevee-lution, you must rename your Eevee before you evolve it. You should log out of the game and log back in, just to make sure the name change is recognized by the Pokémon GO servers.

So, rename your Eevee:

- Sparky for Jolteon
- Rainer for Vaporeon
- Pyro for Flareon

Then, log out of the game; log back in; and check to make sure your name is applied. If so, then evolve your Eevee.

Tip: Run the IV Checker and only evolve your best Eevees.

Pojo Note: The CEO of Niantic teased that there are other Easter Eggs still to be found within the game! Try something wild in the game, maybe you'll be credited with the discovery!

EXPERIENCE VALUES & REWARDS

Experience (or XP) is a unit of measure inside Pokémon GO that tracks your progression through the game. The XP Leveling system in GO is very similar to the system used in the Pokémon role-playing video games. As you gain XP, you will eventually gain levels. Gaining higher levels opens more doors of opportunity for you inside game.

Here are some ways that XP can be gained inside the game.

Pokéstops

Spinning a Pokéstop—50 XP, plus about 3 items

Spinning 10 Unique Pokéstops in a Row—100 XP, 6+ items, and an Egg

Throwing Bonus

Curveball—10 XP

Nice Throw—10 XP

Great Throw—50 XP

Excellent Throw—100 XP

Catching and Evolving Pokémon

Pokémon Caught—100 XP

New Pokémon Caught—500 XP

Evolving Pokémon—500 XP

Hatching Pokémon Eggs

2km Egg—200 XP

5km Egg—500 XP

10km Egg—1,000 XP

Gym Battles

Against Allies—Varies Depending on Ally Level—10 XP to 50 XP

Defeating an Enemy Pokémon at a Gym—100 XP per Pokémon

Bonus for Defeating All Pokémon in a Gym—50 XP

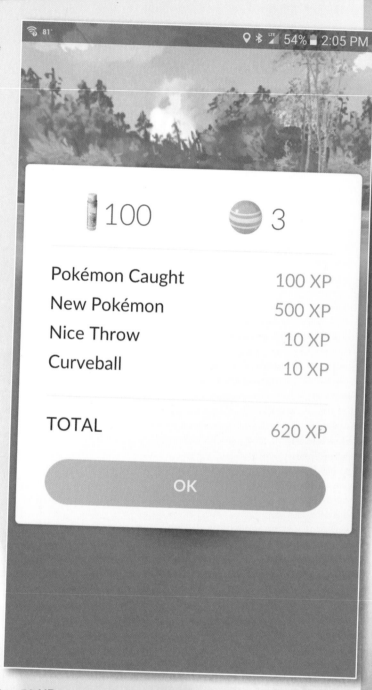

100		3
Pokémon Caught		100 XP
New Pokémon		500 XP
Nice Throw		10 XP
Curveball		10 XP
TOTAL		620 XP

OK

POKÉMON GO WEARABLES

Given how much walking Pokémon GO asks of you, it's no wonder the game is now being integrated into a variety of wearables.

The Pokémon GO Plus is a portable device that will enable Pokémon GO players to enjoy the game even while they're not looking at their mobile devices. The GO Plus connects to a smartphone via Bluetooth and notifies the player about events in the game—such as the appearance of a Pokémon nearby—using LED and vibration. In addition, players can catch Pokémon or perform other simple actions by pressing the button on the device.

Nintendo claims you will be able to collect Pokéballs, Razz Berries, Pokémon Eggs, and other items at set Pokéstop locations without having to look at your smartphone.

It appears the Pokémon GO Plus is worn as a bracelet, but also has a pocket clip. The device will cost you about $35 when it eventually hits streets—Niantic says it will be available "in most countries" on September 16, 2016.

On September 7, 2016, Apple announced support for Pokémon GO on the Apple Watch. Aside from some changes to the interface necessitated by the Watch's smaller screen size, the game play should function roughly the same way. You can expect pop-up notifications about achievements you've reached, and also the ability to track your Egg hatches as you're walking.

We expect that Pokémon GO will soon be coming to Android Wear as well!

MAXIMUM WALKING SPEED

The speed at which you're moving comes into play a couple of ways while playing Pokémon GO: the speed you travel while hatching Eggs, and the speed you travel while searching for Pokémon.

Egg Hatching Speed

On Reddit, user Beastamer did some extensive testing on Egg Hatching Speeds. He determined in August 2016 that: "Pokémon GO does not document your speed directly. It logs your current location (Point A), and then in 1 minute it logs your new location (Point B). It then draws a straight line/"crow's flight" between Point A and Point B and calculates the distance. If this distance is 175 meters or less, you get full credit for the distance you traveled."

What does this mean? Well, basically that the maximum speed you can travel while hatching Eggs is about 6.5 mph. The average person walks 3 mph. The average person rides a bike about 10 mph. The average skater goes about 8 mph. And obviously a car is usually traveling faster than 6.5 mph. Walking is the sweet spot. All of these other methods might work against you, so keep that in mind if you are trying to hatch your Eggs.

Pokémon Searching Speed

In August 2016, Niantic increased the scan refresh rate in Pokémon GO from 5 seconds to 10 seconds. The company claimed this would help ease demand on their servers. The scan refresh rate is how often your phone pings the servers to see where Pokémon are in the world in relation to your GPS. Remember, you have to be within about 100 feet of a Pokémon for it to spawn.

So what does this mean to you? This might not sound like a big deal, and it isn't really if you are walking. But this makes it more challenging to discover Pokémon while biking, skateboarding, or riding in a car. Before the update, the 5 second refresh rate allowed players on bikes to hear the audible sound of Pokémon in their area popping onto their map. Now bikers will probably pass by several Pokémon without the Pokémon even registering.

There is even worse if you are the passenger in a car. The refresh rate makes it rare for Pokémon to spawn on your map while you are driving at normal speeds.

We guess that Niantic really wants you to walk to hatch Eggs and discover Pokémon. Maybe that keeps everyone safer anyway!

Egg Incubator
A device that incubates an Egg as you walk until it is ready to hatch. Breaks after 3 uses.

EXCHANGE FOR 150

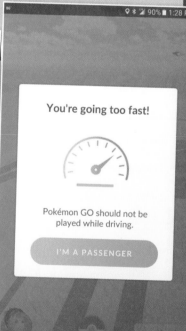

You're going too fast!

Pokémon GO should not be played while driving.

I'M A PASSENGER

BATTERIES AND GLOVES

It was reported that sales of backup batteries had doubled during the summer of 2016 thanks to Pokémon GO. People were hunting for hours at a time and didn't want the fun to end. If your battery dies, your hunt is over!

There is a plethora of backup batteries on the market. Some of the batteries are actually shaped like Pokéballs! I must agree they look cool, but they would be ridiculous to hunt with. Are you supposed to hold the Pokéball in one hand, and your smartphone in the other? How are you going to catch Pokémon that way?

There are two good battery options for longer hunts. One is a detachable cell phone case that doubles as a backup battery. Boostcase makes a cool one for iPhones. The Boostcase only costs about $25 at Amazon, gets great reviews, and doubles your battery life! There are so many makers of Android phones that it's tough to recommend specific battery cases for Androids.

The other option we like are small portable battery chargers that are light and easy to stick in a pocket. Anker is a solid company we trust. They make a lipstick-type charger called a PowerCore+ mini that fits easily in your pocket, and adds over one full charge to an iPhone 6 and Samsung S6.

Winter Is Coming!

People are going to continue to play Pokémon GO over the winter, especially if the Generation II Pokémon from Gold and Silver are released as soon as expected. You are going to be holding your phone in one hand and capturing Pokémon with the other, so you need to keep those fingers warm! If you live in an area where it gets cold over the winter, you might want to look into touchscreen gloves.

Touchscreens work through the electric charge your skin gives off. Touchscreen gloves usually have stainless-steel thread (or other metals) sewn into the fingertips to allow electrical charge to pass through the gloves.

We recommend getting some touchscreen gloves now, before there's a huge run on them unlike any other winter before!

POKÉMON NESTS

As people played Pokémon GO, players started stumbling into Pokémon Nests.

What is a Pokémon Nest?

A Pokémon Nest is a small area with a high concentration of one type of Pokémon, a place you can farm that one specific Pokémon—guaranteed. You can probably farm about 5-8 per hour on average.

Nests would become very popular with the locals if an uncommon Pokémon, such as Charmander, Bulbasaur, Squirtle, Dratini, or Ponyta, spawned there. Basically anything you really need a major quantity of to evolve into something powerful.

As word of mouth spread, folks started exchanging Nest Data online. It has grown so large that you can easily find Pokémon Nest maps on the Internet by just Googling for them.

What are Nests like?

We have visited several Nests while we've been playing Pokémon GO. They include a Magikarp Nest, a Voltorb Nest, a Magnemite Nest, a Machop Nest, a Geodude Nest, and a Charmander Nest. Everyone wants a Charizard!

The most popular Nest we visited was the Charmander Nest in Streamwood, IL, about 35 miles northwest of downtown Chicago. The Nest site is in a little forest preserve area called Bode Lake. There is parking for about 50 cars there and it probably wasn't a popular spot to hang out...*until Pokémon GO hit.*

Five of us decided to have a little picnic there on a Saturday afternoon in August 2016 to check out the fuss. We brought a cooler with drinks, food, a Frisbee, lawn chairs, and back-up batteries. When we pulled up, we realized this was the right spot, because there was nowhere left to park. It was a very hot day, with temperatures in the 90s, but that didn't stop anyone. As soon as we got out of the car, we head someone yell "Charmander," and then we saw about

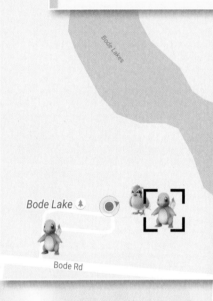

100 people walking to a remote tree in the middle of the field. Now that's what we're talking about! We all rushed off and caught the Charmander and settled back in for out Pokémon picnic.

Well, people kept piling in to the parking lot. All the spots were taken up, so people just started parking anywhere they could around the perimeter. A Forest Preserve sherriff showed up in an SUV and parked in the middle of the field. But there was never any trouble. Just about 150 people working as a team to collect Charmander.

We did this for about two hours that Saturday afternoon, and saw 10 Charmander. Those little buggers are tough to catch. I think I caught seven. We met great people from Wisconsin, Southern Illinois, and even Iowa while we visited. Some people planned to be there all day until they had enough Charmander to evolve into a Charizard.

Now, before you run out to a Nest, keep in mind that Pokémon at Nests can change. This happened in late July and late August 2016. Tangela Nests became Cubone Nests; Geodude Nests became Machop Nests; etc. So, if you decide to go on a Pokémon picnic, first check updated maps online before you venture out and find you're tracking the wrong Pokémon.

Pojo Note: There has been a lot of discussion on message boards about Pokémon caught at Nests having very low IVs. It seems Nests will give you a lot of Candy, but probably not a super strong Pokémon. For that, you'll probably have to hatch one, or catch one away from a Nest.

This book is not sponsored, endorsed by, or otherwise affiliated with any companies or the products featured in the book. This is not an official publication.

63

POKÉMON TYPE ATTACK CHART

"Rock-Paper-Scizors"

Battling in Pokémon is a lot like playing a giant version of "Rock-Paper-Scissors." All Pokémon and their moves are assigned certain Types.

Each Type has strengths and weaknesses against other Types that affect the outcomes of their attacks and defense.

When attacking, you want to use attacks that give you a Type Advantage over your opponent. If an Attack Type is strong against the defending Pokémon's Type, it will be Super Effective and do bonus damage (1.25x normal damage). If an Attack Type is weak against the defending Pokémon's Type, it will be Not Very Effective and do less damage (0.8x normal damage).

In Pokémon there are 18 Pokémon Types to contend with. Some matchups are simple to figure out: Water Attacks are strong against Fire Pokémon, and Fire Attacks are strong versus Grass Pokémon. But when it comes to Types like Bug, Psychic, Ghost, and Fairy, you may be left scratching your head.

So we've included here a simple Combat Chart. The Types in the middle are weak to the Types on the left, and strong against the Types on the right. Build your team accordingly!

Example of Using This Chart:

The Gym you are attacking has a Ninetales. You flip to the Pokédex in the back of the book and you see that Ninetales is a Fire Type Pokémon.

Pokémon Combat Chart (Type Chart)

Weaker Than >	Gym Defender Pokemon Type	Stronger Than >
Fire, Flying, Rock	Bug	Dark, Grass, Psychic
Bug, Fairy, Fighting	Dark	Ghost, Psychic
Dragon, Fairy, Ice	Dragon	Dragon
Ground	Electric	Flying, Water
Poison, Steel	Fairy	Dark, Dragon, Fighting
Fairly, Flying, Psychic	Fighting	Dark, Ice, Normal, Rock, Steel
Ground, Rock, Water	Fire	Bug, Grass, Ice, Steel
Electric, Ice, Rock	Flying	Bug, Fight, Grass
Dark, Ghost	Ghost	Ghost, Psychic
Bug, Fire, Flying, Ice, Poison	Grass	Ground, Rock, Water
Grass, Ice, Water	Ground	Electric, Fire, Poison, Rock, Steel
Fighting, Fire, Rock, Steel	Ice	Dragon, Flying, Grass, Ground
Fighting, Ghost	Normal	None
Ground, Psychic	Poison	Fairy, Grass
Bug, Dark, Ghost	Psychic	Fighting, Poison
Fight, Grass, Ground, Steel, Water	Rock	Bug, Fire, Flying, Ice
Fight, Fire, Ground	Steel	Fairy, Ice, Rock
Electric, Grass	Water	Fire, Ground, Rock

You look for Fire in the Gym Defender Pokémon Type Chart. You see that Fire is Weaker than Ground, Rock, and Water. If you attack Ninetales with one of these types of attacks, your attacks will be Super Effective. You will do 25% more damage.

You also see that Fire is Stronger than Bug, Steel, Grass, and Ice. If you use these types of attacks against Ninetales, your attacks will be Not Very Effective. You will do 20% less damage.

You want to use your Type Advantage at all times possible. You should use your Ground, Rock, or Water Attacks to take down Ninetales. And you should try to match those attacks to those types of Pokémon. So you should attack with someone like Golem or Seaking (whoever is your strongest of these types of Pokémon with Ground, Rock, or Water Attacks).

Some Pokémon, like Rhydon, are actually two Types (Rhydon is both Ground and Rock). That can come in handy at times when attacking, but that also leaves him doubly exposed when defending. If a Pokémon has two Types, both are applied to determine the damage bonus of an attack. For example, Paras has the Bug and Grass Types, which are both weak to Fire. If Paras is hit by a Fire attack, the Fire attack does 56% more damage for being extra Super Effective! (1.25 x 1.25 = 1.5625 or ~56% more)

Just because a Pokémon is a certain Type doesn't mean its moves will also be that type. So always check their moves! The Rhyhorn shown here is a Ground/Rock Pokémon, but his two moves are actually Fighting and Normal (even though one is called Rock Smash)!

Another thing to know is that Pokémon can earn a "Same Type Attack Bonus," or STAB. As the name implies, this increases the power of the move if the attacking Pokémon has the same Type as the move it is using. For example, if a Water Type Pokémon like Squirtle (shown here) uses a Water Type move like "Aqua Jet," the attack will be amplified by 25%! Take advantage of STAB whenever you can.

Last, remember that Gym defender attacks on your Pokémon follow the same rules. Pay attention to your Pokémon Types and your opponent's Types so you don't get caught taking Super Effective attacks on your Pokémon.

Pojo Note: For old-school Pokémon RPG players— there are no Type immunities in Pokémon GO, unlike in the main RPG series. Any immunity just becomes Not Very Effective. Also note that Super Effective bonuses and Not Very Effective penalties are smaller in GO than in the RPG.

POKÉMON GO POWER RANKING CHARTS

Top 20 Pokémon for Defending Gyms

It is difficult to hold Gyms for very long, but these guys can give you the best chance. Their high HP, Attacks, and Defense make them your best bet against the variety of Types out there. Try to get their top Movesets listed in the Pokédex.

1. Lapras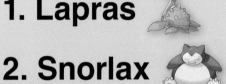

2. Snorlax

3. Dragonite

4. Poliwrath

5. Exeggutor

6. Slowbro

7. Arcanine

8. Venusaur

9. Vaporeon

10. Vileplume

11. Muk

12. Nidoqueen

13. Rhydon

14. Victreebel

15. Golem

16. Hypno

17. Wigglytuff

18. Charizard

19. Clefable

20. Omasta

Pojo Note: We are not listing Legendary Pokémon because none are available at the time of this writing, but all of them would be near the top of this list. These Pokémon rankings could change over time as the Pokémon Company balances attacks inside the game.

Top 20 Pokémon for Attacking

These are ideal for taking down Gyms. Try to get their top Movesets listed in the Pokédex. Always remember to use Type Advantage whenever possible!

1. Snorlax

2. Lapras

3. Vaporeon

4. Exeggutor

5. Arcanine

6. Dragonite

7. Slowbro

8. Venusaur

9. Victreebel

10. Alakazam

11. Poliwrath

12. Omastar

13. Nidoqueen

14. Charizard

15. Vileplume

16. Muk

17. Clefable

18. Rhydon

19. Golem

20. Ninetales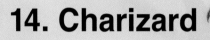

Pojo Note: We are not listing Legendary Pokémon because none are available at the time of this writing, but all of them would be near the top of this list. These Pokémon rankings could change over time as the Pokémon Company balances attacks inside the game.

Strongest Attackers by Type

If you are looking for pure Type Advantage, here are the Top 3 Offensive Pokémon for every Type. Remember, the Attack Type determines Type Advantage over other Pokémon, not the attacking Pokémon's Type, so check your Pokémon's Movesets as well. Check out Pojo's Pokédex, Top 25 Basic Moves Chart, and Top 25 Charged Moves Chart to learn about the most effective moves in battle!

Bug—Super Effective versus Dark, Grass, and Psychic		
1. Venomoth	2. Pinsir	3. Scyther

Runners-Up: Butterfree and Beedrill

Dark—Super Effective against Ghost and Psychic

Pojo Note: There are no Dark Type Pokémon in Generation I. Dark Types were introduced in Generation II. Dark Type moves are in the game, however (Bite, Dark Pulse, Feint Attack, Night Slash, Sucker Punch).

Dragon—Super Effective versus Dragon		
1. Dragonite	2. Dragonair	3. Dratini

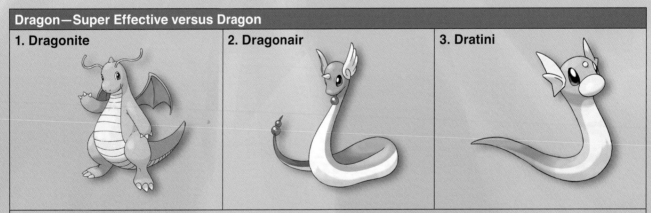

Pojo Note: These are the only 3 Dragon Pokémon in Generation I. Kingdra, an evolution of Seadra, is a strong Dragon Type in Generation II.

Electric—Super Effective versus Flying and Water

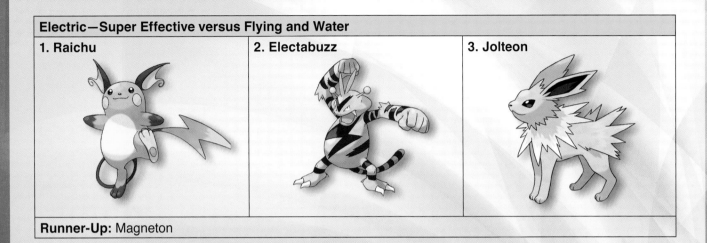

| 1. Raichu | 2. Electabuzz | 3. Jolteon |

Runner-Up: Magneton

Fairy—Super Effective versus Dark, Dragon, and Fighting

| 1. Wigglytuff | 2. Clefable | 3. Mr. Mime |

Pojo Note: There are no other good Fairy Pokémon in Generation I. Generation II will bring us Togetic, Azumarill, and Granbull.

Fighting—Super Effective versus Dark, Ice, Normal, Rock, and Steel

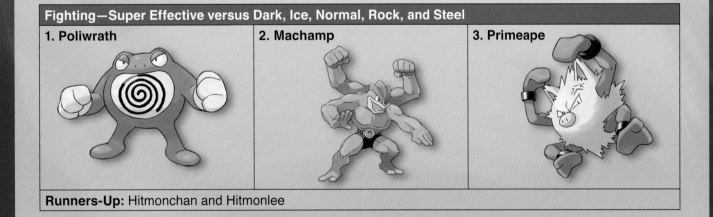

| 1. Poliwrath | 2. Machamp | 3. Primeape |

Runners-Up: Hitmonchan and Hitmonlee

Fire—Super Effective versus Bug, Grass, Ice, and Steel

1. Arcanine

2. Charizard

3. Flareon

Runners-Up: Ninetales, Magmar, and Rapidash

Flying—Super Effective versus Bug, Fighting, and Grass

1. Dragonite

2. Gyarados

3. Charizard

Runners-Up: Scyther, Aerodactyl, and Pidgeot

Ghost—Super Effective versus Ghost and Psychic

1. Gengar

2. Haunter

3. Gastly

Pojo Note: These are the only Ghost Pokémon in Generation I. Misdreavus joins this group in Generation II.

Grass—Super Effective versus Ground, Rock, and Water

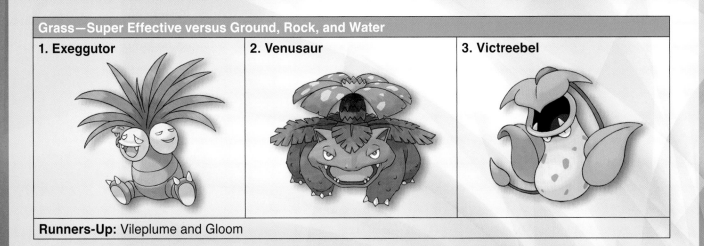

1. Exeggutor

2. Venusaur

3. Victreebel

Runners-Up: Vileplume and Gloom

Ground—Super Effective versus Electric, Fire, Poison, Rock, and Steel

1. Nidoqueen

2. Golem

3. Nidoking

Runners-Up: Rhydon and Marowak

Ice—Super Effective versus Dragon, Flying, Grass, and Ground

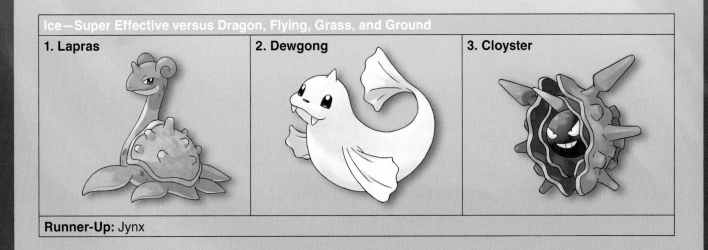

1. Lapras

2. Dewgong

3. Cloyster

Runner-Up: Jynx

Normal—Doesn't have a Type Advantage

1. Snorlax	2. Wigglytuff	3. Kangaskhan

Runners-Up: Pidgeot, Tauros, Dodrio, and Lickitung

Poison—Super Effective versus Fairy and Grass

1. Muk	2. Venusaur	3. Nidoqueen
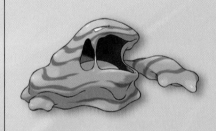		

Runners-Up: Vileplume, Nidoking, and Victreebel

Psychic—Super Effective versus Fighting and Poison

1. Exeggutor	2. Slowbro	3. Alakazam

Runners-Up: Hypno and Starmie

Rock—Super Effective versus Bug, Fire, Flying and Ice

1. Rhydon
2. Golem
3. Omastar

Runner-Up: Aerodactyl

Steel—Super Effective versus Fairy, Ice, and Rock

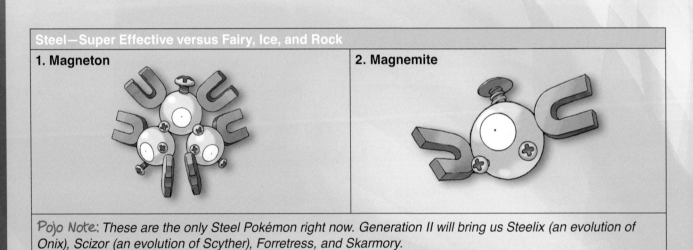

1. Magneton
2. Magnemite

Pojo Note: *These are the only Steel Pokémon right now. Generation II will bring us Steelix (an evolution of Onix), Scizor (an evolution of Scyther), Forretress, and Skarmory.*

Water—Super Effective versus Fire, Ground, and Rock

1. Lapras
2. Vaporeon
3. Golduck

Runners-Up: Slowbro, Starmie, Blastoise, Poliwrath, and Gyarados. (There are a lot of good Water Pokémon out there! Defend your gyms accordingly.)

This book is not sponsored, endorsed by, or otherwise affiliated with any companies or the products featured in the book. This is not an official publication.

73

Top 25 Basic Moves

Basic Moves (or Quick Moves) are the moves you use while tapping the screen when attacking Gyms. When you look at a Pokémon in the Pokédex, it is the top move listed for that Pokémon. Using these moves will power up your Special/Charged Moves. Good Basic Moves are useful for defending Pokémon in Gyms as well.

Here are the Top 25 Moves and their Damage Per Second (DPS). Remember, your Pokémon gets a Same Type Attack Bonus if their Type matches the Attack Type. This increases the damage by 25% in Pokémon GO. Note that your Pokémon's level and stats, including IVs, also affect the damage done by each move, so a low CP Pokémon with fantastic moves will do less damage than a high CP Pokémon with ordinary moves. Check out the Pokédex in the back of the book to learn about the best moves for each Pokémon!

Name	Type	DPS
Pound	Normal	13.0
Metal Claw	Steel	12.7
Psycho Cut	Psychic	12.3
Scratch	Normal	12.0
Water Gun	Water	12.0
Bite	Dark	12.0
Dragon Breath	Dragon	12.0
Wing Attack	Flying	12.0
Fire Fang	Fire	11.9
Shadow Claw	Ghost	11.6
Feint Attack	Dark	11.5
Zen Headbutt	Psychic	11.4
Poison Jab	Poison	11.4
Steel Wing	Steel	11.3
Bug Bite	Bug	11.1
Frost Breath	Ice	11.1
Mud Slap	Ground	11.1
Mud Shot	Ground	10.9
Tackle	Normal	10.9
Bubble	Water	10.9
Vine Whip	Grass	10.8
Ice Shard	Ice	10.7
Rock Smash	Fighting	10.6
Cut	Normal	10.6
Poison Sting	Poison	10.4

Top 25 Charged Moves

Charged Moves (or Special Moves) are the moves you use once your energy bar is filled when attacking Gyms. You hold your finger down on the screen for a full second to release them. When you look at a Pokémon in the Pokédex, it will be the second move listed for that Pokémon. Using these moves will use up the blue bar in Gyms while attacking. Good Charged Moves are useful for defending Pokémon in Gyms as well.

Here are the Top 25 Moves and their Damage Per Second (DPS). Remember, your Pokémon gets a Same Type Attack Bonus if their Type matches the Attack Type. This increases the damage by 25% in Pokémon GO. Note that your Pokémon's level and stats, including IVs, also affect the damage done by each move, so a low CP Pokémon with fantastic moves will do less damage than a high CP Pokémon with ordinary moves. Check out the Pokédex in the back of this book to learn about the best moves for each Pokémon!

Name	Type	DPS
Cross Chop	Fighting	30.0
Stone Edge	Rock	25.8
Body Slam	Normal	25.6
Blizzard	Ice	25.6
Power Whip	Grass	25.0
Megahorn	Bug	25.0
Hurricane	Flying	25.0
Solar Beam	Grass	24.5
Fire Blast	Fire	24.4
Hyper Beam	Normal	24.0
Earthquake	Ground	23.8
Hydro Pump	Water	23.7
Thunder	Electric	23.3
Dragon Claw	Dragon	21.9
Gunk Shot	Poison	21.7
Sludge Bomb	Poison	21.2
Heat Wave	Fire	21.1
Moonblast	Fairy	20.7
Sludge Wave	Poison	20.6
Thunderbolt	Electric	20.4
Petal Blizzard	Grass	20.3
Leaf Blade	Grass	19.6
Psychic	Psychic	19.6
Aqua Tail	Water	19.2
Flamethrower	Fire	19.0

POJO'S POKÉMON GO POKÉDEX

INTRODUCTION

Our detailed Pojo's Pokédex will help your quest to be the very best in Pokémon GO! It will help you catch Pokémon by informing you about how common they are, how easy they are to catch, and how likely they are to flee. Evolution lines will help you decide if you want to evolve certain Pokémon. The Pokédex is especially useful for choosing which Pokémon to train for Gym battles, including information about Pokémon Types, Attacks, and overall power. Certain Pokémon are simply better than others too, and we grade each Pokémon on how good it is for battles. Taking the right Pokémon with you will definitely impact your winning or losing.

The Pokédex is a comprehensive Pokémon encyclopedia that contains a database of statistics on all Pokémon. The Pokédex is used in both the Pokémon video games and in the Pokémon Anime, and now it's being put to use in Pokémon GO. The statistics in the Pokédex vary in each game depending on which factors are most important in that game. These statistics can include: Type, Height, Weight, Evolutions, Attacks, etc. Every single Pokémon in the game has a reference in the Pokédex. Statistics used in Pojo's Pokédex are explained below.

Inside Pokémon GO, the Pokédex shows which Pokémon you have seen and which Pokémon you have caught. If you haven't seen a specific numbered Pokémon, there will be no information about that Pokémon except its shadow. Detailed information about each Pokémon is added to the Pokédex as you catch them.

There are currently 729 Pokémon in the Pokémon Universe (with more coming in Sun & Moon in late 2016). Over the last 20 years, there have been 6 generations of Pokémon with a 7th coming soon:

- Generation I: Red, Blue, Yellow
- Generation II: Gold, Silver, Crystal
- Generation III: Ruby, Sapphire
- Generation IV: Diamond, Pearl, Platinum
- Generation V: Black, White, Black 2, White 2
- Generation VI: X, Y
- Generation VII: Sun, Moon (Coming Soon)

Pokémon GO currently has the 151 Pokémon from Generation I, which were originally found in the very first Pokémon video games. We expect the Pokémon Company to slowly add in more Pokémon to Pokémon GO, Generation by Generation. Our Pokédex is focused on Generation I Pokémon.

POJO'S POKÉDEX STATISTICS

Type – Each Pokémon has 1-2 Types. If its Attack Type matches its Pokémon Type, those attacks will do 25% extra damage (called a Same Type Attack Bonus, or STAB). A Pokémon's Type also determines which attack types will be Super Effective (25% more damage) or Not Very Effective (20% less damage) against them. Consult with the "Pokémon Combat Chart" in this book to help you understand effective Type matchups before you head into Gym battles!

Pojo Note: If a Pokémon has two Types, both are applied to determine the damage bonus of an attack.

For example, Paras has the Bug and Grass Types, which are both weak to Fire. If Paras is hit by a Fire attack, it does 56% more damage for being extra Super Effective! (1.25 x 1.25 = 1.5625 or ~56% more)

Evolves Into – This lists the possible evolutions of the Pokémon and the number of Candies needed to evolve. Some Pokémon (like the starting Pokémon Bulbasaur), evolve twice: first into a Stage 1 Pokémon (Ivysaur) and then into a Stage 2 Pokémon (Venusaur). Others evolve only once, and some do not evolve at all. A few special Pokémon like Eevee can evolve into multiple different versions.

Rarity in the Wild – This is your odds of finding the Pokémon in the wild.

- Everywhere: More than 10% Encounter Rate
- Very Common: 2%-10% Encounter Rate
- Common: 1.20%-1.99% Encounter Rate
- Uncommon: 0.21%-1.19% Encounter Rate
- Rare: 0.01%-0.20% Encounter Rate
- Extremely Rare: Less than 0.01% Encounter Rate – Most Stage 2 Pokémon and Non-Evolving Basic Pokémon fall into this category
- Legendary: 0% chance to find in the wild.

Pojo Note: These are average rarities across the globe. However, there are different spawn rates in different locations. I had Tangela spawn next to my house several times per day, but others players I know still haven't even seen one. There are also "Nest Sites" where multiples of uncommon Pokémon can spawn. You can find these Nest maps by searching on Google. You may have seen hundreds of Doduos in your neighborhood, while others may never see them. Part of the fun of Pokémon GO is exploring to find new areas with different Pokémon! Keep that in mind as you read the Pokédex.

Flee Rates – Every Pokémon has a built-in Flee Rate. For instance, Abra has the highest Flee Rate in the Game: 99% if you don't catch it on the first throw. Most Rare Pokémon will actually stick around and battle you for a while though!

- Very High: 20%+ Flee Rate
- High: 10%-20% Flee Rate
- Moderate: 8%-9% Flee Rate
- Low: 6%-7% Flee Rate
- Very Low: 5% or Less Flee Rate

Capture Rates – Every Pokémon also has a built-in Capture Rate. Magikarp is very easy to catch. Over ½ your throws with a regular Pokéball will snag you a Magikarp. Charizard has a very low capture rate. Less than 5% of your throws with a regular Pokéball will snag you a Charizard. You can increase your odds of catching Pokémon though by using Razz Berries and better Pokéballs. Your Trainer Level and the Pokémon's level will also affect your capture rate. Rare Pokémon with very low capture rates just might run you out of Pokéballs!

- Very High: 40%+ Capture Rate
- High: 20%-39% Capture Rate
- Moderate: 16%-19% Capture Rate
- Low: 10%-15% Capture Rate
- Very Low: 9% or Less Capture Rate

Max CP: As we mentioned earlier in the book, CP is Combat Power. Each Pokémon you catch will be assigned a CP. Our Pokédex lists the Maximum Combat Power for Each Pokémon. The maximum Pokémon level at the time we wrote this book was Level 30.

Best Basic Moves: The highest DPS (Damage Per Second) basic moves your Pokémon can learn, including the same type attack bonus. This can be very important for Gym battles and hopefully future one on one battles against friends. Best moves go from left to right.

Best Charged Moves: The highest DPS Charged Move your Pokémon can learn, including the same attack bonus. This can be very important for Gym battles. If an attack is not listed, it's probably not a great attack. Best moves go from left to right in the Pokédex.

Pojo Note: Regarding Moves – Remember that when you evolve a Pokémon, its moves will change and it may learn different Movesets.

Pojo's Pokémon Rating: This is our overall assessment of the Pokémon. We graded all Pokémon using a standard academic grading system: A, B, C, D, and F (from highest to lowest). Plus and minus grades are being given as well.

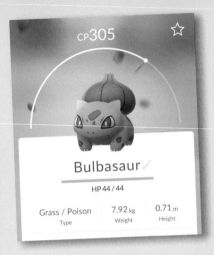

#1 BULBASAUR C-

Type: Grass / Poison

Evolves Into: Ivysaur (25 candies)

Rarity in the Wild: Uncommon

Flee Rate: High

Capture Rate: Moderate

Max CP: 1072

Best Basic Moves: Vine Whip, Tackle

Best Charged Moves: Power Whip, Seed Bomb

Comments and Fun Facts: The best use of Bulbasaur is to catch him and evolve him into Venusaur. Run the IV checker and keep only your best ones. When you get 125 candies, evolve your best Bulbasaur straight into a Venusaur. You might want to research Bulbasaur Nest sites. This applies to all Basic Pokémon that can evolve two more times.

#2 IVYSAUR C

Type: Grass / Poison

Evolves Into: Venusaur (100 candies)

Rarity in the Wild: Rare

Flee Rate: Low

Capture Rate: Very Low

Max CP: 1632

Best Basic Moves: Vine Whip, Razor Leaf

Best Charged Moves: Solar Beam, Sludge Bomb

Comments and Fun Facts: A Stage 1 that you should evolve into Venusaur. Run the IV checker and keep only your best ones.

#3 Venusaur A-

Type: Grass / Poison

Evolves Into: Does Not Evolve

Rarity in the Wild: Extremely Rare

Flee Rate: Very Low

Capture Rate: Very Low

Max CP: 2580

Best Basic Moves: Vine Whip, Razor Leaf

Best Charged Moves: Petal Blizzard, Solar Beam, Sludge Bomb

Comments and Fun Facts: Venusaur is a force to be reckoned with. It makes a great Gym defender, and is also great at attacking Gyms as well. The "Venus" in "Venusaur" is thought to reflect the Venus Flytrap on its back.

#4 Charmander C-

Type: Fire

Evolves Into: Charmeleon (25 candies)

Rarity in the Wild: Uncommon

Flee Rate: High

Capture Rate: Moderate

Max CP: 955

Best Basic Moves: Scratch, Ember

Best Charged Moves:
Flamethrower, Flame Burst

Comments and Fun Facts:
The best use of Charmander is to catch him and evolve him into Charizard. Run the IV checker and keep only your best ones. When you get 125 candies, evolve your best Charmander straight into a Charizard.

#5 Charmeleon C

Type: Fire

Evolves Into: Charizard (100 candies)

Rarity in the Wild: Rare

Flee Rate: Low

Capture Rate: Very Low

Max CP: 1557

Best Basic Moves: Ember, Scratch

Best Charged Moves: Fire Punch, Flame Burst

Comments and Fun Facts:
Charmeleon is a blending of the words "Char" and "Chameleon". A Stage 1 Pokémon you should evolve into Charizard.

#6 Charizard A-

Type: Fire

Evolves Into: Does Not Evolve

Rarity in the Wild: Extremely Rare

Flee Rate: Very Low

Capture Rate: Very Low

Max CP: 2602

Best Basic Moves: Ember, Wing Attack

Best Charged Moves:
Flamethrower, Fire Blast

Comments and Fun Facts:
Charizard is a blending of the words "Char" and "Lizard". His Japanese name is "Lizardon". Charizard took the No. 1 spot in IGN's "Top 100 Pokémon" list in 2011. A Base Set 1st Edition Charizard card can fetch up to $5,000 on eBay.

#7 Squirtle C-

Type: Water

Evolves Into: Wartortle (25 candies)

Rarity in the Wild: Uncommon

Flee Rate: High

Capture Rate: Moderate

Max CP: 1009

Best Basic Moves: Bubble, Tackle

Best Charged Moves: Aqua Tail, Aqua Pulse

Comments and Fun Facts: Catch Squirtles to evolve one into Blastoise. Run the IV checker and keep only your best ones. When you get 125 candies, evolve your best Squirtle straight into a Blastoise.

#8 Wartortle C

Type: Water

Evolves Into: Blastoise (100 candies)

Rarity in the Wild: Rare

Flee Rate: Low

Capture Rate: Very Low

Max CP: 1583

Best Basic Moves: Water Gun, Bite

Best Charged Moves: Hydro Pump, Ice Beam

Comments and Fun Facts: A Stage 1 Pokémon that you should evolve into Blastoise. Run the IV checker and keep only your best ones.

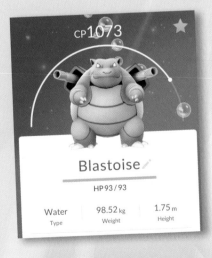

#9 Blastoise A

Type: Water

Evolves Into: Does Not Evolve

Rarity in the Wild: Extremely Rare

Flee Rate: Very Low

Capture Rate: Very Low

Max CP: 2542

Best Basic Moves: Water Gun, Bite

Best Charged Moves: Hydro Pump, Ice Beam

Comments and Fun Facts: Blastoise is like a turtle blended with a tank, and his name is a blend of a "tortoise" and the "blast" from a tank's canon.

#10 Caterpie F

Type: Bug

Evolves Into: Metapod (12 candies)

Rarity in the Wild: Very Common

Flee Rate: Very High

Capture Rate: Very High

Max CP: 444

Best Basic Moves: Bug Bite, Tackle

Best Charged Moves: Struggle

Comments and Fun Facts: The best use of Caterpie is to catch him and evolve him into Butterfree. Caterpie is pretty darn common, so this shouldn't be too difficult. Because he only takes 12 candies to evolve, you can also evolve a bunch of Caterpies for XP. This is the first Pokémon Ash catches in the anime.

#11 Metapod F

Type: Bug

Evolves Into: Butterfree (50 candies)

Rarity in the Wild: Uncommon

Flee Rate: Moderate

Capture Rate: High

Max CP: 478

Best Basic Moves: Bug Bite, Tackle

Best Charged Moves: Struggle

Comments and Fun Facts: Metapod is a Cocoon Pokémon that "struggles" to do anything useful. Keep your best and evolve it into Butterfree.

#12 Butterfree C+

Type: Bug / Flying

Evolves Into: Does Not Evolve

Rarity in the Wild: Extremely Rare

Flee Rate: Low

Capture Rate: Low

Max CP: 1455

Best Basic Moves: Bug Bite, Confusion

Best Charged Moves: Bug Buzz, Psychic, Signal Beam

Comments and Fun Facts: Butterfree isn't all that great of a Pokémon in GO, but with the abundance of Caterpie, it's a pretty good Stage 2 Pokémon early in the game until you eventually get better ones.

#13 WEEDLE F

Type: Bug / Poison
Evolves Into: Kakuna (12 candies)
Rarity in the Wild: Very Common
Flee Rate: Very High
Capture Rate: Very High
Max CP: 449

Best Basic Moves: Bug Bite, Poison Sting

Best Charged Moves: Struggle

Comments and Fun Facts: One use of Weedle is to catch him and evolve him into Beedrill. Weedle is pretty darn common, so this shouldn't be too difficult. You can also evolve lots of them for easy XP.

#14 KAKUNA F

Type: Bug / Poison
Evolves Into: Beedrill (50 candies)
Rarity in the Wild: Uncommon
Flee Rate: Moderate
Capture Rate: High
Max CP: 485

Best Basic Moves: Bug Bite, Poison Sting

Best Charged Moves: Struggle

Comments and Fun Facts: Don't waste Pokeballs on the evolved forms of common Pokemon. They can be tough to catch, and don't award you any special bonus for being evolved.

#15 BEEDRILL C+

Type: Bug / Poison
Evolves Into: Does Not Evolve
Rarity in the Wild: Rare
Flee Rate: Low
Capture Rate: Low
Max CP: 1229
Best Basic Moves: Bug Bite, Poison Jab

Best Charged Moves: Sludge Bomb, X-Scissor

Comments and Fun Facts: Beedrill is a kind of sister-type Pokémon to Butterfree. Both are pretty easy to get via evolutions. And neither is very good in Pokémon GO once you get your heavy hitters.

#16 PIDGEY D-

Type: Normal / Flying

Evolves Into: Pidgeotto (12 candies)

Rarity in the Wild: Everywhere

Flee Rate: High

Capture Rate: High

Max CP: 680

Best Basic Moves: Tackle, Quick Attack

Best Charged Moves: Twister, Aerial Ace, Air Cutter

Comments and Fun Facts: Pidgeys are everywhere, just like pigeons in big cities. The best way to use them is to evolve lots of them for easy XP. Store enough candies to evolve lots of Pokémon, and then pop a Lucky Egg and evolve them all to double the XP! Check their IVs too so you can evolve the best ones into Pidgeot.

#17 PIDGEOTTO C-

Type: Normal / Flying

Evolves Into: Pidgeot (50 candies)

Rarity in the Wild: Uncommon

Flee Rate: Moderate

Capture Rate: High

Max CP: 1224

Best Basic Moves: Wing Attack, Steel Wing

Best Charged Moves: Twister, Aerial Ace, Air Cutter

Comments and Fun Facts: Run the IV checker and keep only your best ones. Evolve into Pidgeot when you get enough candies. This is the 2nd Pokémon Ash catches in the anime.

#18 PIDGEOT C+

Type: Normal / Flying

Evolves Into: Does Not Evolve

Rarity in the Wild: Uncommon

Flee Rate: Low

Capture Rate: Low

Max CP: 2091

Best Basic Moves: Wing Attack, Steel Wing

Best Charged Moves: Hurricane, Aerial Ace, Air Cutter

Comments and Fun Facts: An easy Stage 2 Pokémon to evolve due to the abundance of Pidgey. But overall, not a great Pokémon in GO.

#19 Rаттата D-

Type: Normal

Evolves Into: Raticate (25 candies)

Rarity in the Wild: Everywhere

Flee Rate: Very High

Capture Rate: Very High

Max CP: 582

Best Basic Moves: Tackle

Best Charged Moves: Body Slam, Hyper Fang

Comments and Fun Facts: Rattata are great for power leveling. Catch a ton of them. Get over 250 candy. Keep 10 Rattata in your inventory. Pop a Lucky Egg, and evolve all 10 in a row. This works with all the Pokémon you see everywhere.

#20 Rатicate C

Type: Normal

Evolves Into: Does Not Evolve

Rarity in the Wild: Uncommon

Flee Rate: Low

Capture Rate: Moderate

Max CP: 1444

Best Basic Moves: Bite, Quick Attack

Best Charged Moves: Hyper Beam, Hyper Fang

Comments and Fun Facts: If you're good at dodging, then Raticate can be a strong attacker. Otherwise, it has very weak defense and will be easily knocked out in battle.

#21 Spearow D-

Type: Normal / Flying

Evolves Into: Fearow (50 candies)

Rarity in the Wild: Very Common

Flee Rate: High

Capture Rate: Very High

Max CP: 687

Best Basic Moves: Peck, Quick Attack

Best Charged Moves: Drill Peck, Aerial Ace

Comments and Fun Facts: Spearows are everywhere, just like sparrows in big cities. Keep the best ones and evolve into Fearow. Turn the rest into candy and evolve a few for XP.

#22 Fearow C

Type: Normal / Flying

Evolves Into: Does Not Evolve

Rarity in the Wild: Rare

Flee Rate: Low

Capture Rate: Moderate

Max CP: 1746

Best Basic Moves: Steel Wing, Peck

Best Charged Moves: Drill Run, Aerial Ace, Twister

Comments and Fun Facts: Fearow's name seems to be a blend of "fear" and "sparrow". Not a very good Pokémon in GO.

#23 Ekans D-

Type: Poison

Evolves Into: Arbok (50 candies)

Rarity in the Wild: Very Common

Flee Rate: High

Capture Rate: Very High

Max CP: 824

Best Basic Moves: Poison Sting, Acid

Best Charged Moves: Gunk Shot, Sludge Bomb

Comments and Fun Facts: "Ekans" is "snake" spelled backwards.

#24 Arbok C

Type: Poison

Evolves Into: Does Not Evolve

Rarity in the Wild: Rare

Flee Rate: Low

Capture Rate: Moderate

Max CP: 1767

Best Basic Moves: Bite, Acid

Best Charged Moves: Gunk Shot, Sludge Wave

Comments and Fun Facts: "Arbok" is "cobra" spelled backwards, with k instead of c. Not a very good Pokémon in GO.

This book is not sponsored, endorsed by, or otherwise affiliated with any companies or the products featured in the book. This is not an official publication.

85

#25 Pikachu C-

Type: Electric

Evolves Into: Raichu (50 candies)

Rarity in the Wild: Rare

Flee Rate: High

Capture Rate: Moderate

Max CP: 888

Best Basic Moves: Thunder Shock, Quick Attack

Best Charged Moves: Thunder, Thunderbolt

Comments and Fun Facts: Pikachu is the Official Mascot of Pokémon. "Pika" is the Japanese word for the noise of crackling lightning. "Chu" is the Japanese word for the sound a mouse makes. Pikachu is Ash's starting Pokémon in the anime, and has been with Ash in every episode since 1997. In 2008, a new protein that helps with vision was discovered in Japan. They named the protein: Pikachurin. It's "lightning-fast" with "shocking-like" electrical effects.

#26 Raichu B+

Type: Electric

Evolves Into: Does Not Evolve

Rarity in the Wild: Extremely Rare

Flee Rate: Low

Capture Rate: Very Low

Max CP: 2028

Best Basic Moves: Spark, Thundershock

Best Charged Moves: Thunder, Thunderpunch

Comments and Fun Facts: In the first season of the anime, Ash was given a Thunder Stone, and had an opportunity to evolve his Pikachu into Raichu. Ash refused. You shouldn't refuse though: Raichu is much better in Pokémon GO! Raichu is one of the best Electric Attackers in the game right now.

#27 Sandshrew D

Type: Ground

Evolves Into: Sandslash (50 candies)

Rarity in the Wild: Uncommon

Flee Rate: High

Capture Rate: Very High

Max CP: 799

Best Basic Moves: Mud Shot, Scratch

Best Charged Moves: Dig, Rock Tomb

Comments and Fun Facts: Sandshrew is based on a mammal called a Pangolin. Pangolins curl up into a balls, have sharp claws, and live in deserts.

#28 Sandslash C

Type: Ground

Evolves Into: Does Not Evolve

Rarity in the Wild: Rare

Flee Rate: Low

Capture Rate: Moderate

Max CP: 1810

Best Basic Moves: Mud Shot, Metal Claw

Best Charged Moves: Earthquake, Rock Tomb, Bulldoze

Comments and Fun Facts: Not a very good Pokémon in GO for a final form.

#29 Nidoran♀ D-

Type: Poison

Evolves Into: Nidorina (25 candies)

Rarity in the Wild: Common

Flee Rate: High

Capture Rate: Very High

Max CP: 876

Best Basic Moves: Poison Sting, Bite

Best Charged Moves: Sludge Bomb

Comments and Fun Facts: Nidorina were the only Pokémon in Generation I to come in both female (♀) and male (♂) forms. The best use of Nidoran♀ is to catch her and evolve her into Nidoqueen. Run the IV checker and keep only your best ones. When you get 125 candies, evolve your best Nidoran♀ straight into a Nidoqueen.

#30 Nidorina C-

Type: Poison

Evolves Into: Nidoqueen (100 candies)

Rarity in the Wild: Rare

Flee Rate: Low

Capture Rate: High

Max CP: 1405

Best Basic Moves: Poison Sting, Bite

Best Charged Moves: Sludge Bomb, Poison Fang

Comments and Fun Facts: The female Nidoran line is blue and the male Nidoran line is pink. While this sounds backwards to many people today, before World War II most Western cultures considered blue the more suitable color for girls and pink the stronger masculine color for boys. Keep only your best Nidorina after running the IV checker and evolve into Nidoqueen when you get enough candies.

CP1201

Nidoqueen

HP 104 / 104

Poison / Ground	50.3 kg	1.3 m
Type	Weight	Height

#31 Nidoqueen

Type: Poison / Ground

Evolves Into: Does Not Evolve

Rarity in the Wild: Extremely Rare

Flee Rate: Very Low

Capture Rate: Low

Max CP: 2485

Best Basic Moves: Poison Jab

Best Charged Moves: Earthquake, Stone Edge, Sludge Wave

Comments and Fun Facts: Nidoqueen is a very good Gym defender. Nidoqueen and Nidoking are the only Pokémon with Poison/Ground type combinations.

CP59

Nidoran♂

HP 22 / 22

Poison	9.62 kg	0.52 m
Type	Weight	Height

#32 Nidoran♂

Type: Poison

Evolves Into: Nidorino (25 candies)

Rarity in the Wild: Common

Flee Rate: High

Capture Rate: Very High

Max CP: 843

Best Basic Moves: Poison Sting

Best Charged Moves: Body Slam

Comments and Fun Facts: Nidorans were the only Pokémon in Generation I to come in both male (♂) and female (♀) forms. The best use of Nidoran♂ is to catch him and evolve him into Nidoking. Run the IV checker and keep only your best ones. When you get 125 candies, evolve your best Nidoran straight into a Nidoking.

CP110

Nidorino

HP 32 / 32

Poison	14.38 kg	0.72 m
Type	Weight	Height

#33 Nidorino C-

Type: Poison

Evolves Into: Nidoking (100 candies)

Rarity in the Wild: Rare

Flee Rate: Low

Capture Rate: High

Max CP: 1373

Best Basic Moves: Poison Sting, Poison Jab

Best Charged Moves: Sludge Bomb, Horn Attack

Comments and Fun Facts: The male Nidoran line is pink and the female Nidoran line is blue. While this sounds backwards to many people today, before World War II most Western cultures considered pink the stronger masculine color for boys and blue the more suitable dainty color for girls. Keep only your best Nidorino after running the IV checker and evolve into Nidoking when you get enough candies.

#34 NIDOKING A-

Type: Poison / Ground

Evolves Into: Does Not Evolve

Rarity in the Wild: Extremely Rare

Flee Rate: Very Low

Capture Rate: Low

Max CP: 2475

Best Basic Moves: Poison Jab, Fury Cutter

Best Charged Moves: Earthquake, Sludge Wave, Megahorn

Comments and Fun Facts: Nidoking is a good Gym attacker, as well a good Gym defender. Nidoqueen and Nidoking are the only Pokémon with Poison/Ground type combinations.

#35 CLEFAIRY D

Type: Normal

Evolves Into: Clefable (50 candies)

Rarity in the Wild: Rare

Flee Rate: High

Capture Rate: High

Max CP: 1201

Best Basic Moves: Pound, Zen Headbutt

Best Charged Moves: Moonblast, Body Slam

Comments and Fun Facts: Clefairy was almost the face of Pokémon. Clefairy was originally going to be the official Pokémon Mascot. Clefairy was the star of the original Manga. At the last minute, they changed the mascot to Pikachu. Phew!

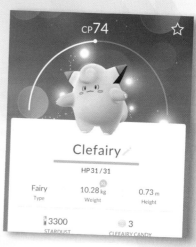

#36 CLEFABLE B+

Type: Normal

Evolves Into: Does Not Evolve

Rarity in the Wild: Extremely Rare

Flee Rate: Low

Capture Rate: Very Low

Max CP: 2398

Best Basic Moves: Zen Headbutt, Pound

Best Charged Moves: Dazzling Gleam, Moonblast, Psychic

Comments and Fun Facts: Clefable makes for a pretty good Gym defender in GO.

#37 Vulpix D

Type: Fire

Evolves Into: Ninetales (50 candies)

Rarity in the Wild: Rare

Flee Rate: High

Capture Rate: High

Max CP: 831

Best Basic Moves: Ember, Quick Attack

Best Charged Moves: Flamethrower, Body Slam

Comments and Fun Facts: Vulpix is a fox Pokémon with six curled tails, based on the Japanese fox spirit kitsune. According to Japanese folklore, all foxes have the ability to shape shift into human form.

#38 Ninetales B-

Type: Fire

Evolves Into: Does Not Evolve

Rarity in the Wild: Extremely Rare

Flee Rate: Low

Capture Rate: Very Low

Max CP: 2188

Best Basic Moves: Ember, Feint Attack

Best Charged Moves: Fire Blast, Flamethrower

Comments and Fun Facts: Not a great Pokémon in GO, but still a cool Pokémon to add to your Pokédex, and fairly good early in your GO career if you find one.

#39 Jigglypuff D

Type: Normal

Evolves Into: Wigglytuff (50 candies)

Rarity in the Wild: Uncommon

Flee Rate: High

Capture Rate: Very High

Max CP: 918

Best Basic Moves: Pound, Feint Attack

Best Charged Moves: Body Slam, Play Rough

Comments and Fun Facts: In the anime, Jigglypuff loves to perform for a crowd, but gets angry when her Sing attack puts everyone to sleep and retaliates by drawing funny faces on the sleepers. Jigglypuff is an unlockable character in Super Smash Bros, a great fighting game on the Nintendo 64, and is also available in the sequels Melee (GameCube) and Brawl (Wii).

#40 Wigglytuff A-

Type: Normal
Evolves Into: Does Not Evolve
Rarity in the Wild: Extremely Rare
Flee Rate: Low
Capture Rate: Moderate
Max CP: 2177

Best Basic Moves: Pound, Feint Attack
Best Charged Moves: Hyper Beam, Play Rough
Comments and Fun Facts: Wigglytuff makes for a pretty good attacker with Pound and Hyper Beam.

#41 Zubat D

Type: Poison / Flying
Evolves Into: Golbat (50 candies)
Rarity in the Wild: Everywhere
Flee Rate: Very High
Capture Rate: Very High
Max CP: 643
Best Basic Moves: Quick Attack, Bite

Best Charged Moves: Sludge Bomb, Poison Fang, Air Cutter
Comments and Fun Facts: Zubat has a high flee rate and a high capture rate, if you manage to hit him. It's somewhat hard to hit him with a Pokéball as he is very small and moves around the screen so much. If you miss, there's a good chance he's gone. Since they take 50 candies to evolve, feel free to ignore them.

#42 Golbat C-

Type: Poison / Flying
Evolves Into: Crobat in Generation II
Rarity in the Wild: Uncommon
Flee Rate: Low
Capture Rate: Moderate
Max CP: 1921

Best Basic Moves: Wing Attack, Bite
Best Charged Moves: Poison Fang, Air Cutter, Ominous Wind
Comments and Fun Facts: Golbat is still not a very good Pokémon, but we expect its next evolution, Crobat, in Generation II to be pretty good. So keep farming that Zubat candy.

#43 Oddish D

Type: Grass / Poison

Evolves Into: Gloom (25 candies)

Rarity in the Wild: Common

Flee Rate: High

Capture Rate: Very High

Max CP: 1148

Best Basic Moves: Razor Leaf, Acid

Best Charged Moves: Sludge Bomb, Seed Bomb

Comments and Fun Facts: This "odd" "radish" is actually based on the mandrake plant, a toxic plant from the Mediterranean that was commonly used in medieval medicine and magic. According to legend, mandrake roots shrieked when pulled out of the ground, killing all who heard them.

#44 Gloom C-

Type: Grass / Poison

Evolves Into: Vileplume (100 candies), and Bellossom in Generation II

Rarity in the Wild: Rare

Flee Rate: Low

Capture Rate: High

Max CP: 1689

Best Basic Moves: Razor Leaf, Acid

Best Charged Moves: Petal Blizzard, Sludge Bomb

Comments and Fun Facts: In the anime, Gloom's notorious stench was Gym Leader Erika's secret weapon. Ash overcame the stink and saved Erika's Gloom from a fire in the Gym, earning his Rainbow Badge. Run the IV checker and keep only your best ones. When you get enough candies, evolve your best into Vileplume. Maybe save a good one to evolve into Bellossom when Generation II comes out.

#45 Vileplume A-

Type: Grass / Poison

Evolves Into: Does Not Evolve

Rarity in the Wild: Extremely Rare

Flee Rate: Very Low

Capture Rate: Low

Max CP: 2493

Best Basic Moves: Razor Leaf, Acid

Best Charged Moves: Petal Blizzard, Solar Beam

Comments and Fun Facts: Vileplume is a very good Gym defender, and a pretty good Gym attacker.

#46 Paras D

Type: Bug / Grass

Evolves Into: Parasect (50 candies)

Rarity in the Wild: Very Common

Flee Rate: High

Capture Rate: Very High

Max CP: 917

Best Basic Moves: Bug Bite, Fury Cutter

Best Charged Moves: Seed Bomb, X-Scissor

Comments and Fun Facts: Remember back in the introduction of this book we told you that the creator of Pokémon was a bug lover? Well, Paras actually looks like an immature Cicada in real life. And it has been infected with Tochukaso Mushrooms. The mushroom parasites are living in harmony with Paras as the host.

#47 Parasect C

Type: Bug / Grass

Evolves Into: Does Not Evolve

Rarity in the Wild: Rare

Flee Rate: Low

Capture Rate: Moderate

Max CP: 1747

Best Basic Moves: Bug Bite, Fury Cutter

Best Charged Moves: Solar Beam, X-Scissor

Comments and Fun Facts: Do you see how Paras has eyes and Parasect does not? Supposedly, when Paras becomes Parasect, the mushroom parasite has taken over as the host and controls the Pokémon. Spooky! This real life phenomenon is due to *Cordyceps* fungus. Many different types of *Cordyceps* infect a variety of insects and control their brains.

#48 Venonat D

Type: Bug / Poison

Evolves Into: Venomoth (50 candies)

Rarity in the Wild: Common

Flee Rate: High

Capture Rate: Very High

Max CP: 1029

Best Basic Moves: Bug Bite, Confusion

Best Charged Moves: Signal Beam, Poison Fang

Comments and Fun Facts: "Venom" "Gnat" is good for one thing ... evolving.

CP 241

Venomoth

HP 42 / 42

Bug / Poison	12.71 kg	1.66 m
Type	Weight	Height

#49 Venomoth C

Type: Bug / Poison

Evolves Into: Does Not Evolve

Rarity in the Wild: Rare

Flee Rate: Low

Capture Rate: Moderate

Max CP: 1890

Best Basic Moves: Bug Bite, Confusion

Best Charged Moves: Bug Buzz, Psychic

Comments and Fun Facts: "Venom" "Moth" isn't a very good Pokémon in the long run, but can be useful attacking Gyms when you're first starting out.

CP 38

Diglett

HP 10 / 10

Ground	0.79 kg	0.19 m
Type	Weight	Height

#50 Diglett D

Type: Ground

Evolves Into: Dugtrio (50 candies)

Rarity in the Wild: Uncommon

Flee Rate: High

Capture Rate: Very High

Max CP: 457

Best Basic Moves: Mud Shot, Scratch

Best Charged Moves: Dig, Mud Bomb

Comments and Fun Facts: It is revealed in Pokémon Mystery Dungeon that Diglett has feet!

CP 461

Dugtrio

HP 42 / 42

Ground	33.3 kg	0.74 m
Type	Weight	Height

#51 Dugtrio C

Type: Ground

Evolves Into: Does Not Evolve

Rarity in the Wild: Extremely Rare

Flee Rate: Low

Capture Rate: Moderate

Max CP: 1169

Best Basic Moves: Mud Shot, Sucker Punch

Best Charged Moves: Earthquake, Stone Edge

Comments and Fun Facts: It is made by sticking 3 Digletts together, but it weighs more than 10x as much? Dugtrio and Magneton are two Pokémon that evolve by pasting 3 of the Base Level Pokémon together. You don't need more than one Pokémon on hand to evolve, though. Not a good Pokémon to use in GO, but still nice to add to your Pokédex.

#52 MEOWTH D

Type: Normal

Evolves Into: Persian (50 candies)

Rarity in the Wild: Uncommon

Flee Rate: High

Capture Rate: Very High

Max CP: 756

Best Basic Moves: Scratch, Bite

Best Charged Moves: Body Slam, Night Slash

Comments and Fun Facts: Meowth is somewhat the opposite of Pikachu. Pikachu is #25, Meowth is #52. Pikachu is considered a good Pokémon in the anime, while Meowth is a member of the villainous Team Rocket. They are Cat & Mouse, kind of like the old Tom & Jerry cartoons.

#53 PERSIAN C

Type: Normal

Evolves Into: Does Not Evolve

Rarity in the Wild: Rare

Flee Rate: Low

Capture Rate: Moderate

Max CP: 1632

Best Basic Moves: Scratch, Feint Attack

Best Charged Moves: Play Rough, Night Slash, Power Gem

Comments and Fun Facts: Not a good attacker or defender in GO, but nice to add to your Pokédex.

#54 PSYDUCK D

Type: Water

Evolves Into: Golduck (50 candies)

Rarity in the Wild: Uncommon

Flee Rate: High

Capture Rate: Very High

Max CP: 1110

Best Basic Moves: Water Gun, Zen Headbutt

Best Charged Moves: Psybeam, Aqua Tail

Comments and Fun Facts: Misty's psychic duck seems to be a dimwit in the Pokémon Anime, but can explode with tremendous Psychic Power.

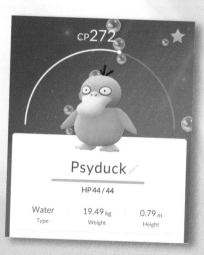

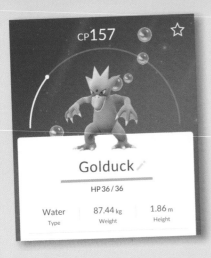

#55 Golduck

Type: Water

Evolves Into: Does Not Evolve

Rarity in the Wild: Rare

Flee Rate: Low

Capture Rate: Moderate

Max CP: 2387

Best Basic Moves: Water Gun, Confusion

Best Charged Moves: Hydro Pump, Ice Beam, Psychic

Comments and Fun Facts: A Golduck with Water Gun/Hydro Pump is an awesome attacker and not a bad Gym defender either.

#56 Mankey D

Type: Fighting

Evolves Into: Primeape (50 candies)

Rarity in the Wild: Uncommon

Flee Rate: High

Capture Rate: Very High

Max CP: 879

Best Basic Moves: Scratch, Karate Chop

Best Charged Moves: Cross Chop, Brick Break

Comments and Fun Facts: In the anime, a wild Mankey steals and wears Ash's signature Pokémon League Expo hat, which Ash claimed to have "sent in about a million postcards" to win. Team Rocket ticks off the Mankey, and it evolves into Primeape. Ash captures it just after it evolves to Primeape.

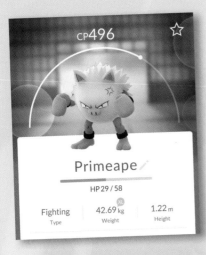

#57 Primeape C

Type: Fighting

Evolves Into: Does Not Evolve

Rarity in the Wild: Rare

Flee Rate: Low

Capture Rate: Moderate

Max CP: 1865

Best Basic Moves: Low Kick, Karate Chop

Best Charged Moves: Cross Chop, Low Sweep

Comments and Fun Facts: Not a great Pokémon in GO. Just evolve a Mankey and fill your Pokédex.

#58 Growlithe D

Type: Fire

Evolves Into: Arcanine (50 candies)

Rarity in the Wild: Uncommon

Flee Rate: High

Capture Rate: High

Max CP: 1335

Best Basic Moves: Bite, Ember

Best Charged Moves: Flamethrower, Body Slam

Comments and Fun Facts: In the anime, James of Team Rocket had a pet Growlithe named Growlie when he was as a child. He left it behind when he ran away from home.

#59 Arcanine A+

Type: Fire

Evolves Into: Does Not Evolve

Rarity in the Wild: Extremely Rare

Flee Rate: Low

Capture Rate: Very Low

Max CP: 2984

Best Basic Moves: Fire Fang, Bite

Best Charged Moves: Fire Blast, Flamethrower, Bulldoze

Comments and Fun Facts: Was originally going to be a Legendary Pokémon. He's even named a Legendary Pokémon in some video games and in the anime, but he's not considered a Legendary Pokémon. Either way, he's pretty darn strong. He has the 2nd strongest DPS in the game after Dragonite (after eliminating the all Legendary Pokémon).

#60 Poliwag D-

Type: Water

Evolves Into: Poliwhirl (25 candies)

Rarity in the Wild: Common

Flee Rate: High

Capture Rate: Very High

Max CP: 796

Best Basic Moves: Bubble, Mud Shot

Best Charged Moves: Body Slam, Wrap

Comments and Fun Facts: Poliwag's swirl pattern is meant to look like the visible intestines of tadpoles.

#61 POLIWHIRL C-

Type: Water

Evolves Into: Poliwrath (100 candies), and Politoed in Generation II

Rarity in the Wild: Rare

Flee Rate: Low

Capture Rate: High

Max CP: 1340

Best Basic Moves: Bubble, Mud Shot

Best Charged Moves: Scald, Mud Bomb

Comments and Fun Facts: Run the IV checker and keep only your best ones. When you get enough candies, evolve your best into a Poliwrath.

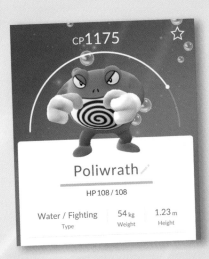

#62 POLIWRATH A+

Type: Water / Fighting

Evolves Into: Does Not Evolve

Rarity in the Wild: Extremely Rare

Flee Rate: Very Low

Capture Rate: Low

Max CP: 2505

Best Basic Moves: Bubble, Mud Shot

Best Charged Moves: Hydro Pump, Submission, Ice Punch

Comments and Fun Facts: Poliwrath is the 2nd best Gym defender right now, behind Lapras!

#63 ABRA D

Type: Psychic

Evolves Into: Kadabra (25 candies)

Rarity in the Wild: Uncommon

Flee Rate: Very, Very High

Capture Rate: Very High

Max CP: 600

Best Basic Moves: Zen Headbutt

Best Charged Moves: Psyshock, Signal Beam

Comments and Fun Facts: Abra has the highest Flee Rate in the Game (99%). Use a Razz Berry and your best Pokéball and pray to the Pokégods! If he busts out, he's most likely gone. This is reminiscent of Abra's habit of instantly teleporting away in the video games.

#64 Kadabra C-

Type: Psychic

Evolves Into: Alakazam (100 candies)

Rarity in the Wild: Extremely Rare

Flee Rate: Low

Capture Rate: High

Max CP: 1132

Best Basic Moves: Psycho Cut, Confusion

Best Charged Moves: Dazzling Gleam, Psybeam

Comments and Fun Facts: In November 2000, Uri Geller, a man who claims to be a psychic (and claims he can bend spoons with psychic powers), tried to sue Nintendo for $90 million claiming that Kadabra was an unauthorized parody of Geller. His case must have been pretty good, as Kadabra hasn't appeared in the Pokémon Trading Card game since 2003! Kadabra still appears in video games though.

#65 Alakazam B+

Type: Psychic

Evolves Into: Does Not Evolve

Rarity in the Wild: Extremely Rare

Flee Rate: Very Low

Capture Rate: Low

Max CP: 1814

Best Basic Moves: Psycho Cut, Confusion

Best Charged Moves: Psychic, Dazzling Gleam, Shadow Ball

Comments and Fun Facts: Alakazam's Psycho Cut is a very good Basic Move to spam when attacking.

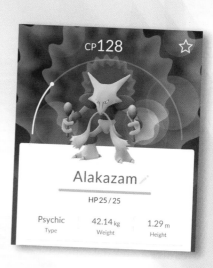

#66 Machop D

Type: Fighting

Evolves Into: Machoke (25 candies)

Rarity in the Wild: Uncommon

Flee Rate: High

Capture Rate: Very High

Max CP: 1090

Best Basic Moves: Low Kick, Karate Chop

Best Charged Moves: Cross Chop, Brick Break

Comments and Fun Facts: The best use of Machop is to catch him and evolve him into Machamp. Run the IV checker and keep only your best ones. When you get 125 candies, evolve your best Machop straight into a Machamp.

This book is not sponsored, endorsed by, or otherwise affiliated with any companies or the products featured in the book. This is not an official publication.

99

#67 MACHOKE C-

Type: Fighting

Evolves Into: Machamp (100 candies)

Rarity in the Wild: Rare

Flee Rate: Low

Capture Rate: High

Max CP: 1761

Best Basic Moves: Low Kick, Karate Chop

Best Charged Moves: Cross Chop, Brick Break

Comments and Fun Facts: From the Pokémon Handbook: "Sometimes it's too busy looking at itself in the mirror to train".

#68 MACHAMP B-

Type: Fighting

Evolves Into: Does Not Evolve

Rarity in the Wild: Extremely Rare

Flee Rate: Very Low

Capture Rate: Low

Max CP: 2594

Best Basic Moves: Karate Chop, Bullet Punch

Best Charged Moves: Stone Edge, Cross Chop

Comments and Fun Facts: Machamp isn't all that great in Pokémon GO right now. In the Trading Card Game, it is believed there are more Machamps than any other 1st Edition foil rares in Base Set 1. This is because they were in every Starter Set that everyone bought. A gem mint "10" copy will still fetch $200 on eBay though.

#69 BELLSPROUT D

Type: Grass / Poison

Evolves Into: Weepinbell (25 candies)

Rarity in the Wild: Common

Flee Rate: High

Capture Rate: Very High

Max CP: 1117

Best Basic Moves: Vine Whip, Acid

Best Charged Moves: Sludge Bomb, Power Whip

Comments and Fun Facts: Catch a bunch and evolve him into Victreebel. Run the IV checker and keep only your best ones. When you get 125 candies, evolve your best Bellsprout straight into a Victreebel.

#70 WEEPINBELL

Type: Grass / Poison

Evolves Into: Victreebel (100 candies)

Rarity in the Wild: Rare

Flee Rate: Low

Capture Rate: High

Max CP: 1724

Best Basic Moves: Razor Leaf, Acid

Best Charged Moves: Power Whip, Sludge Bomb

Comments and Fun Facts: Weepinbell and Victreebel are both based on pitcher plants. Pitcher plants are carnivorous plants that eat insects. Their secret lies in their juice which is not actually nectar, but the smell is enticing to bugs. The juice contains chemicals that are similar to those found in your stomach. Those juices slowly eat and swallow the skin of its prey until it dissolves the prey completely, becoming the very juice that it once tried to drink. And you thought it didn't look scary.

#71 VICTREEBEL B+

Type: Grass / Poison

Evolves Into: Does Not Evolve

Rarity in the Wild: Extremely Rare

Flee Rate: Very Low

Capture Rate: Low

Max CP: 2531

Best Basic Moves: Razor Leaf, Acid

Best Charged Moves: Solar Beam, Sludge Bomb, Leaf Blade

Comments and Fun Facts: Victreebel makes for a pretty good Gym attacker.

#72 TENTACOOL D

Type: Water / Poison

Evolves Into: Tentacruel (50 candies)

Rarity in the Wild: Uncommon

Flee Rate: High

Capture Rate: Very High

Max CP: 905

Best Basic Moves: Bubble, Poison Sting

Best Charged Moves: Bubble Beam, Water Pulse

Comments and Fun Facts: Season 1 of the Pokémon anime featured an episode titled: "Tentacool & Tentacruel". The episode was not shown on TV for many years after Tentacruel was shown toppling skyscrapers. It can still be seen on the Season 1 DVD though.

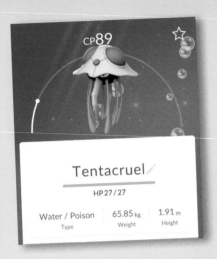

#73 Tentacruel B

Type: Water / Poison

Evolves Into: Does Not Evolve

Rarity in the Wild: Rare

Flee Rate: Low

Capture Rate: Moderate

Max CP: 2205

Best Basic Moves: Poison Jab, Acid

Best Charged Moves: Hydro Pump, Blizzard

Comments and Fun Facts: Tentacruel makes a decent Gym defender. Check our Defender List earlier in the book.

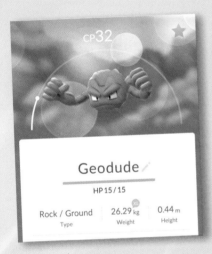

#74 Geodude D

Type: Rock / Ground

Evolves Into: Graveler (25 candies)

Rarity in the Wild: Uncommon

Flee Rate: High

Capture Rate: Very High

Max CP: 849

Best Basic Moves: Rock Throw, Tackle

Best Charged Moves: Rock Slide, Slide

Comments and Fun Facts: The best use of Geodude is to catch him and evolve him into Golem. Run the IV checker and keep only your best ones. When you get 125 candies, evolve your best Geodude straight into a Golem.

#75 Graveler C-

Type: Rock / Ground

Evolves Into: Golem (100 candies)

Rarity in the Wild: Rare

Flee Rate: Low

Capture Rate: High

Max CP: 1434

Best Basic Moves: Rock Throw, Mud Shot

Best Charged Moves: Stone Edge, Rock Slide

Comments and Fun Facts: In Season 1 of the anime, Giselle uses her Graveler to battle Misty's Starmie. She shows Misty and Ash that a Pokémon can still win a battle even it has a type disadvantage, if it's level is high enough. You should keep that in mind for your own Gym battles!

#76 Golem A-

Type: Rock / Ground

Evolves Into: Does Not Evolve

Rarity in the Wild: Extremely Rare

Flee Rate: Very Low

Capture Rate: Low

Max CP: 2303

Best Basic Moves: Rock Throw, Mud Shot

Best Charged Moves: Stone Edge, Earthquake, Ancient Power

Comments and Fun Facts: Golem is a pretty decent attacker and Gym defender in Pokémon GO right now.

#77 Ponyta D

Type: Fire

Evolves Into: Rapidash (50 candies)

Rarity in the Wild: Rare

Flee Rate: High

Capture Rate: Very High

Max CP: 1516

Best Basic Moves: Ember, Tackle

Best Charged Moves: Fire Blast, Flame Charge

Comments and Fun Facts: The Pokémon Stadium Pokédex entry says that Ponyta can jump over the Eiffel Tower!

#78 Rapidash C+

Type: Fire

Evolves Into: Does Not Evolve

Rarity in the Wild: Extremely Rare

Flee Rate: Low

Capture Rate: Low

Max CP: 2199

Best Basic Moves: Ember, Low Kick

Best Charged Moves: Fire Blast, Heat Wave

Comments and Fun Facts: Rapidash is a gorgeous Pokémon, but it's not really good as a Pokémon GO attacker or defender right now.

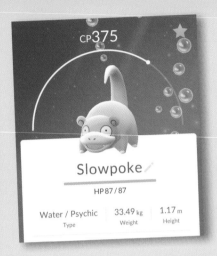

CP375

Slowpoke

HP 87 / 87

Water / Psychic	33.49 kg	1.17 m
Type	Weight	Height

#79 Slowpoke

Type: Water / Psychic

Evolves Into: Slowbro (50 candies), and also Slowking in Generation II

Rarity in the Wild: Uncommon

Flee Rate: High

Capture Rate: Very High

Max CP: 1219

Best Basic Moves: Water Gun, Confusion

Best Charged Moves: Psychic, Psyshock

Comments and Fun Facts: In the Gold & Silver video games, you can evolve a Slowpoke into a Slowking by trading it while it's holding a King's Rock. Slowking has a Shellder on its head, like a crown.

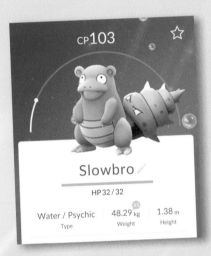

CP103

Slowbro

HP 32 / 32

Water / Psychic	48.29 kg	1.38 m
Type	Weight	Height

#80 Slowbro

Type: Water / Psychic

Evolves Into: Does Not Evolve

Rarity in the Wild: Extremely Rare

Flee Rate: Low

Capture Rate: Moderate

Max CP: 2597

Best Basic Moves: Confusion, Water Gun

Best Charged Moves: Psychic, Ice Beam, Water Pulse

Comments and Fun Facts: Slowpoke evolves into Slowbro when a Shellder bites its tail. If the Shellder were to decide to let go, it would turn back into a Slowpoke. Slowbro is an excellent Pokémon to put in Gyms as a defender.

CP367

Magnemite

HP 32 / 32

Electric / Steel	4.97 kg	0.27 m
Type	Weight	Height

#81 Magnemite

Type: Electric / Steel

Evolves Into: Magneton (50 candies)

Rarity in the Wild: Uncommon

Flee Rate: High

Capture Rate: Very High

Max CP: 891

Best Basic Moves: Spark, Thunder Shock

Best Charged Moves: Thunderbolt, Discharge

Comments and Fun Facts: Magnemite is named for magnetism, one of the key forces of nature, but video game Pokédex entries explain that it hovers in the air because of the very non-real force of antigravity. Magnemite was just an electric Pokémon in Red & Blue, but became an Electric/Steel Pokémon in Gold & Silver.

#82 Magneton D

Type: Electric / Steel

Evolves Into: Magnezone in Generation IV

Rarity in the Wild: Extremely Rare

Flee Rate: Low

Capture Rate: Moderate

Max CP: 1880

Best Basic Moves: Spark, Thunder Shock

Best Charged Moves: Flash Cannon, Discharge

Comments and Fun Facts: Magneton are created by joining 3 Magnemites, but it weighs 10 times more? Dugtrio and Magneton are two Pokémon that evolve by pasting 3 of the Base Level Pokémon together. You don't need more than one Pokémon on hand to evolve, though. Also can evolve into Magnezone in Generation IV Games.

#83 Farfetch'd C-

Type: Normal / Flying

Evolves Into: Does Not Evolve

Rarity in the Wild: Can only be caught in Asia, Extremely Rare

Flee Rate: Moderate

Capture Rate: High

Max CP: 1264

Best Basic Moves: Cut, Fury Cutter

Best Charged Moves: Leaf Blade, Aerial Ace

Comments and Fun Facts: Farfetch'd cannot be caught or hatched in North America. Maybe this will change in the future. But for now, you'd have to travel to Asia to catch one.

#84 Doduo D

Type: Normal / Flying

Evolves Into: Dodrio (50 candies)

Rarity in the Wild: Uncommon

Flee Rate: High

Capture Rate: Very High

Max CP: 855

Best Basic Moves: Peck, Quick Attack

Best Charged Moves: Drill Peck, Aerial Ace

Comments and Fun Facts: Doduo can run faster than it can fly.

#85 Dodrio C

Type: Normal / Flying
Evolves Into: Does Not Evolve
Rarity in the Wild: Rare
Flee Rate: Low
Capture Rate: Moderate
Max CP: 1836

Best Basic Moves: Feint Attack, Steel Wing

Best Charged Moves: Drill Peck, Aerial Ace, Air Cutter

Comments and Fun Facts: Not a very good Pokémon in GO.

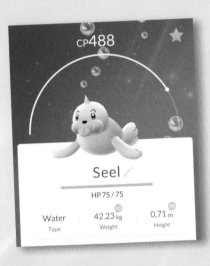

#86 Seel D

Type: Water
Evolves Into: Dewgong (50 candies)
Rarity in the Wild: Uncommon
Flee Rate: Moderate
Capture Rate: Very High
Max CP: 1107

Best Basic Moves: Water Gun, Ice Shard

Best Charged Moves: Aqua Tail, Aqua Jet

Comments and Fun Facts: In Season 1 of the anime, Misty's sisters have Seels for Pokémon.

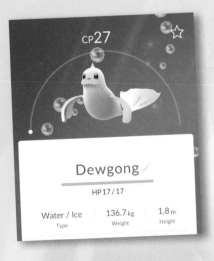

#87 Dewgong

Type: Water / Ice
Evolves Into: Does Not Evolve
Rarity in the Wild: Extremely Rare
Flee Rate: Low
Capture Rate: Moderate
Max CP: 2146

Best Basic Moves: Ice Shard, Frost Breath

Best Charged Moves: Blizzard, Aqua Jet, Icy Wind

Comments and Fun Facts: Real dugongs are not seals at all – they are a type of manatee and live in the oceans near Australia and South Asia. Dewgong is a solid Gym defender.

#88 Grimer D

Type: Poison

Evolves Into: Muk (50 candies)

Rarity in the Wild: Uncommon

Flee Rate: High

Capture Rate: Very High

Max CP: 1284

Best Basic Moves: Acid, Mud Slap

Best Charged Moves: Sludge Bomb, Sludge

Comments and Fun Facts: Reminds us of Grimace from the old McDonald's commercials. In the old days Grimace used to steal milkshakes.

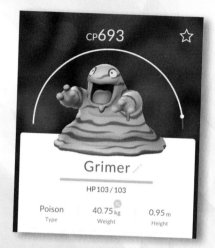

#89 Muk A-

Type: Poison

Evolves Into: Does Not Evolve

Rarity in the Wild: Extremely Rare

Flee Rate: Low

Capture Rate: Moderate

Max CP: 1284

Best Basic Moves: Poison Jab, Acid

Best Charged Moves: Dark Pulse, Sludge Wave, Gunk Shot

Comments and Fun Facts: Muk is a pretty solid all-around Pokémon. He makes for a great Gym defender.

#90 Shellder D

Type: Water

Evolves Into: Cloyster (50 candies)

Rarity in the Wild: Uncommon

Flee Rate: High

Capture Rate: Very High

Max CP: 823

Best Basic Moves: Tackle, Ice Shard

Best Charged Moves: Water Pulse, Bubble Beam

Comments and Fun Facts: Shellder clamps onto a Slowpoke's tail to evolve into Slowbro. Shellder clamps onto a Slowpoke's head to evolve into a Slowking.

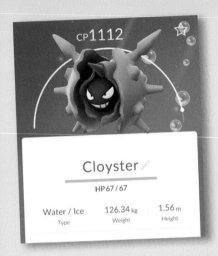

#91 CLOYSTER B+

Type: Water / Ice
Evolves Into: Does Not Evolve
Rarity in the Wild: Extremely Rare
Flee Rate: Low
Capture Rate: Moderate
Max CP: 2053

Best Basic Moves: Frost Breath, Ice Shard
Best Charged Moves: Blizzard, Hydro Pump
Comments and Fun Facts: Cloyster is a very good Gym attacker when Water/Ice is called for.

#92 GASTLY D

Type: Ghost / Poison
Evolves Into: Haunter (25 candies)
Rarity in the Wild: Uncommon
Flee Rate: High
Capture Rate: High
Max CP: 804
Best Basic Moves: Lick, Sucker Punch

Best Charged Moves: Sludge Bomb, Ominous Wind

Comments and Fun Facts: The best use of Gastly in Pokémon GO is to catch him and evolve him into Gengar. Run the IV checker and keep only your best ones. When you get 125 candies, evolve your best Gastly straight into a Gengar.

#93 HAUNTER C-

Type: Ghost / Poison
Evolves Into: Gengar (100 candies)
Rarity in the Wild: Rare
Flee Rate: Low
Capture Rate: Moderate
Max CP: 1380

Best Basic Moves: Shadow Claw, Lick
Best Charged Moves: Sludge Bomb, Shadow Ball

Comments and Fun Facts: Haunter and Gastly are the lightest Pokémon. In the anime, Ash befriends a Haunter in Season 1. But the Haunter is too silly to use in battle, so Ash gives it to Gym Leader Sabrina.

#94 Gengar B+

Type: Ghost / Poison

Evolves Into: Does Not Evolve

Rarity in the Wild: Extremely Rare

Flee Rate: Very Low

Capture Rate: Very Low

Max CP: 2078

Best Basic Moves: Shadow Claw, Sucker Punch

Best Charged Moves: Sludge Wave, Shadow Ball

Comments and Fun Facts: Gengar looks somewhat like a scary Clefable shadow. He is also the same height and weight as Clefable. Gengar has pretty good DPS, but isn't as good in Pokémon GO as he was in Red & Blue. He was Pojo's first personal favorite Pokémon, according to his daughter.

#95 Onix C

Type: Rock / Ground

Evolves Into: Steelix in Generation II

Rarity in the Wild: Extremely Rare

Flee Rate: Moderate

Capture Rate: Moderate

Max CP: 857

Best Basic Moves: Rock Throw, Tackle

Best Charged Moves: Stone Edge, Rock Slide

Comments and Fun Facts: Onix isn't that great of a Pokémon in GO, but he evolves to Steelix in Generation II. So keep your eyes out for a good Onix anyway.

#96 Drowzee D

Type: Psychic

Evolves Into: Hypno (50 candies)

Rarity in the Wild: Common

Flee Rate: High

Capture Rate: Very High

Max CP: 1075

Best Basic Moves: Pound, Confusion

Best Charged Moves: Psychic, Psyshock

Comments and Fun Facts: Drowzee is based on a mammal called a tapir. According to Japanese folklore, tapirs devour dreams and nightmares.

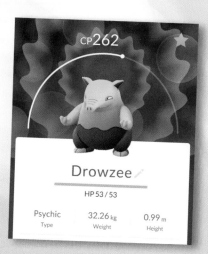

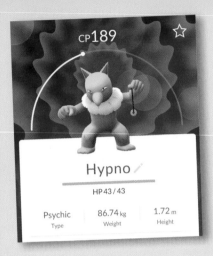

#97 Hypno *B*

Type: Psychic

Evolves Into: Does Not Evolve

Rarity in the Wild: Extremely Rare

Flee Rate: Low

Capture Rate: Moderate

Max CP: 2184

Best Basic Moves: Confusion, Zen Headbutt

Best Charged Moves: Psychic, Psyshock, Shadow Ball

Comments and Fun Facts: Hypno holds a pendulum that is classically used for hypnotizing people. Hypno is actually a pretty decent Gym defender.

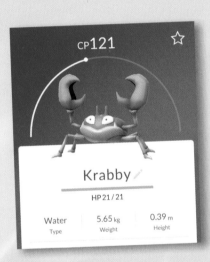

#98 Krabby *D*

Type: Water

Evolves Into: Kingler (50 candies)

Rarity in the Wild: Uncommon

Flee Rate: High

Capture Rate: Very High

Max CP: 792

Best Basic Moves: Bubble, Mud Shot

Best Charged Moves: Vice Grip, Bubble Beam

Comments and Fun Facts: Ash catches one in Season 1 of the anime. This is where Ash learns that a trainer can only carry 6 Pokémon at a time. After he catches Krabby, the Pokéball transfers automatically to Professor Oak.

#99 Kingler *C+*

Type: Water

Evolves Into: Does Not Evolve

Rarity in the Wild: Extremely Rare

Flee Rate: Low

Capture Rate: Moderate

Max CP: 1823

Best Basic Moves: Metal Claw, Mud Shot

Best Charged Moves: X-Scissor, Vice Grip, Water Pulse

Comments and Fun Facts: In the RPGs, Kingler has the highest base stat ATTACK of all non-legendary Pokémon. But for some reason, he isn't good right now in Pokémon GO.

#100 VOLTORB

Type: Electric

Evolves Into: Electrode (50 candies)

Rarity in the Wild: Rare

Flee Rate: High

Capture Rate: Very High

Max CP: 840

Best Basic Moves: Spark, Tackle

Best Charged Moves: Thunderbolt, Discharge

Comments and Fun Facts: Voltorb and Electrode are like living Pokéballs. Voltorb is red on top, while Electrode is red on the bottom.

#101 ELECTRODE C

Type: Electric

Evolves Into: Does Not Evolve

Rarity in the Wild: Extremely Rare

Flee Rate: Low

Capture Rate: Moderate

Max CP: 1646

Best Basic Moves: Spark, Tackle

Best Charged Moves: Thunderbolt, Hyper Beam

Comments and Fun Facts: Electrode isn't a very good Pokémon in GO, but can be used in Gym battles if you don't have any better Electric Pokémon and need the type advantage.

#102 EXEGGCUTE D

Type: Grass / Psychic

Evolves Into: Exeggutor (50 candies)

Rarity in the Wild: Uncommon

Flee Rate: Low

Capture Rate: Very High

Max CP: 1100

Best Basic Moves: Confusion

Best Charged Moves: Psychic, Seed Bomb

Comments and Fun Facts: In the video games, you evolve Exeggcute using a Leaf Stone.

CP1625

Exeggutor

HP 121 / 121

Grass / Psychic	134.47 kg	2.17 m
Type	Weight	Height

#103 Exeggutor

Type: Grass / Psychic

Evolves Into: Does Not Evolve

Rarity in the Wild: Extremely Rare

Flee Rate: Low

Capture Rate: Moderate

Max CP: 2955

Best Basic Moves: Confusion, Zen Headbutt

Best Charged Moves: Solar Beam, Seed Bomb

Comments and Fun Facts: The CEO of the Pokémon Company, Tsunekazu Ishihara, says Exeggutor is his favorite Pokémon. Maybe that's why Exeggutor is one of the best Gym defenders and attackers in Pokémon GO!

CP43

Cubone

HP 18 / 18

Ground	8.51 kg	0.45 m
Type	Weight	Height

#104 Cubone D

Type: Ground

Evolves Into: Marowak (50 candies)

Rarity in the Wild: Uncommon

Flee Rate: High

Capture Rate: High

Max CP: 1007

Best Basic Moves: Mud Slap, Rock Smash

Best Charged Moves: Bone Club, Dig

Comments and Fun Facts: Cubone seems to be a more popular Pokémon in Japan than in North America.

CP666

Marowak

HP 64 / 64

Ground	58.74 kg	1.14 m
Type	Weight	Height

#105 Marowak C

Type: Ground

Evolves Into: Does Not Evolve

Rarity in the Wild: Extremely Rare

Flee Rate: Low

Capture Rate: Low

Max CP: 1657

Best Basic Moves: Mud Slap, Rock Smash

Best Charged Moves: Earthquake, Bone Club

Comments and Fun Facts: Not a very good Pokémon in GO right now.

#106 Hitmonlee C

Type: Fighting

Evolves Into: Does Not Evolve

Rarity in the Wild: Extremely Rare

Flee Rate: Moderate

Capture Rate: Moderate

Max CP: 1493

Best Basic Moves: Rock Smash, Low Kick

Best Charged Moves: Stone Edge, Low Sweep

Comments and Fun Facts: Hitmonlee is thought to have been named for the famous martial artist and actor Bruce Lee in the American version of the game. Not a very good Pokémon to use in GO at this time.

#107 Hitmonchan C

Type: Fighting

Evolves Into: Does Not Evolve

Rarity in the Wild: Extremely Rare

Flee Rate: Moderate

Capture Rate: Moderate

Max CP: 1517

Best Basic Moves: Rock Smash, Bullet Punch

Best Charged Moves: Brick Break, Thunder Punch

Comments and Fun Facts: Hitmonchan is thought to have been named for the famous martial artist and actor Jackie Chan in the American version of the game. Not a very good Pokémon to use in GO at this time.

#108 Lickitung C

Type: Normal

Evolves Into: Lickilicky in Generation IV

Rarity in the Wild: Extremely Rare

Flee Rate: Moderate

Capture Rate: Moderate

Max CP: 1627

Best Basic Moves: Lick, Zen Headbutt

Best Charged Moves: Hyper Beam, Power Whip

Comments and Fun Facts: Lickitung is a Poké Float in Super Smash Bros. You can climb up on it when it rolls out its tongue. Just an average Pokémon in GO.

#109 KOFFING *D*

Type: Poison

Evolves Into: Weezing (50 candies)

Rarity in the Wild: Rare

Flee Rate: High

Capture Rate: Very High

Max CP: 1152

Best Basic Moves: Acid, Tackle

Best Charged Moves: Sludge Bomb, Sludge

Comments and Fun Facts: Koffing and Weezing were named NY and LA in the beta versions of the first game, referencing Air Pollution in New York and Los Angeles. This was changed though just before Red & Blue came out.

#110 Weezing *C*

Type: Poison

Evolves Into: Does Not Evolve

Rarity in the Wild: Extremely Rare

Flee Rate: Low

Capture Rate: Moderate

Max CP: 2250

Best Basic Moves: Acid, Tackle

Best Charged Moves: Sludge Bomb, Shadow Ball

Comments and Fun Facts: Weezing is a nasty Pokéball Pokémon in Super Smash Bros. Melee, using its Poison Gas attack. It's not as nasty Pokémon GO right now though.

#111 RHYHORN *D*

Type: Ground / Rock

Evolves Into: Rhydon (50 candies)

Rarity in the Wild: Rare

Flee Rate: High

Capture Rate: Very High

Max CP: 1182

Best Basic Moves: Mud Slap, Rock Smash

Best Charged Moves: Bulldoze, Horn Attack

Comments and Fun Facts: Nothing special here. Just collect them and evolve to a fairly powerful Rhydon.

#112 Rhydon A-

Type: Ground / Rock

Evolves Into: Rhyperior in Generation IV

Rarity in the Wild: Extremely Rare

Flee Rate: Low

Capture Rate: Moderate

Max CP: 2243

Best Basic Moves: Mud Slap, Rock Smash

Best Charged Moves: Earthquake, Stone Edge, Megahorn

Comments and Fun Facts: Rhydon was the very first Pokémon created by Game Freak (the makers of Pokémon). Rhydon makes for a solid Gym defender.

CP26

Rhydon

HP 19 / 19

| Ground / Rock | 78.55 kg | 1.43 m |
| Type | Weight | Height |

#113 Chansey D

Type: Normal

Evolves Into: Blissey in Generation II

Rarity in the Wild: Extremely Rare

Flee Rate: Moderate

Capture Rate: Moderate

Max CP: 675

Best Basic Moves: Pound, Zen Headbutt

Best Charged Moves: Psychic, Psybeam

Comments and Fun Facts: Chanseys are usually assisting Nurse Joys in the Pokémon Centers in the anime. Chansey is not a very good Pokémon in GO, but will probably evolve into Blissey in Generation II, so keep looking for a good one.

CP502

Chansey

HP 349 / 349

| Normal | 32.6 kg | 1.08 m |
| Type | Weight | Height |

#114 Tangela C

Type: Grass

Evolves Into: Tangrowth in Generation IV

Rarity in the Wild: Extremely Rare

Flee Rate: Moderate

Capture Rate: Moderate

Max CP: 1740

Best Basic Moves: Vine Whip

Best Charged Moves: Solar Beam, Power Whip

Comments and Fun Facts: Tangela is not a very good Pokémon in GO, but will probably evolve into Tangrowth in Generation IV, so keep looking for a good one.

CP738

Tangela

HP 73 / 73

| Grass | 21.24 kg | 0.8 m |
| Type | Weight | Height |

#115 Kangaskhan C

Type: Normal

Evolves Into: Does Not Evolve

Rarity in the Wild: Can only be caught in Australia, Rare

Flee Rate: Moderate

Capture Rate: Moderate

Max CP: 2043

Best Basic Moves: Mud Slap, Low Kick

Best Charged Moves: Earthquake, Brick Break

Comments and Fun Facts: Can only be caught in Australia. It's not a very good Pokémon in GO, so no worries there. In its Mega Kangaskhan form in the video games, the mother appears unchanged but the baby pops out of its pouch and grows spikes and claws and is a feisty competitor.

#116 Horsea D

Type: Water

Evolves Into: Seadra (50 candies)

Rarity in the Wild: Rare

Flee Rate: High

Capture Rate: Very High

Max CP: 795

Best Basic Moves: Water Gun, Bubble

Best Charged Moves: Dragon Pulse, Bubble Beam

Comments and Fun Facts: A seahorse that shoots ink from its snout. You might actually consider saving up a great Horsea and 125 candy, and waiting to evolve it straight into a Kingdra when Generation II comes out.

#117 Seadra B-

Type: Water

Evolves Into: Kingdra in Generation II

Rarity in the Wild: Extremely Rare

Flee Rate: Low

Capture Rate: Moderate

Max CP: 1713

Best Basic Moves: Water Gun, Dragon Breath

Best Charged Moves: Hydro Pump, Blizzard

Comments and Fun Facts: A pretty good Water Attacker in battle, and it might evolve into Kingdra in Generation II. Kingdra might be a beast! Kingdra ranks in the Top 10% of Pokémon in Base Stats in the RPG.

#118 Goldeen D

Type: Water

Evolves Into: Seaking (50 candies)

Rarity in the Wild: Uncommon

Flee Rate: High

Capture Rate: Very High

Max CP: 965

Best Basic Moves: Mud Shot, Peck

Best Charged Moves: Aqua Tail, Water Pulse

Comments and Fun Facts: Goldeen and Seaking may be based on one of the avatars of the Hindu god Vishnu, Matsya, depicted as a fish with a horn.

#119 Seaking C

Type: Water

Evolves Into: Does Not Evolve

Rarity in the Wild: Extremely Rare

Flee Rate: Low

Capture Rate: Moderate

Max CP: 2044

Best Basic Moves: Poison Jab, Peck

Best Charged Moves: Megahorn, Drill Run

Comments and Fun Facts: Not a very good Pokémon in GO right now.

#120 Staryu D

Type: Water

Evolves Into: Starmie

Rarity in the Wild: Uncommon

Flee Rate: High

Capture Rate: Very High

Max CP: 938

Best Basic Moves: Water Gun, Quick Attack

Best Charged Moves: Swift, Bubble Beam

Comments and Fun Facts: In the anime, Staryu is one of Misty's main Pokémon she uses in battles.

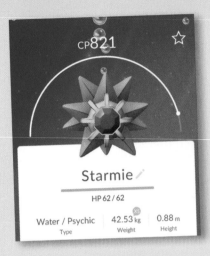

#121 Starmie B+

Type: Water / Psychic

Evolves Into: Does Not Evolve

Rarity in the Wild: Extremely Rare

Flee Rate: Low

Capture Rate: Moderate

Max CP: 2182

Best Basic Moves: Water Gun, Quick Attack

Best Charged Moves: Hydro Pump, Power Gem

Comments and Fun Facts: Starmie is a very good Water/Psychic Pokémon to use when attacking Gyms.

#122 Mr. Mime C

Type: Psychic

Evolves Into: Does Not Evolve

Rarity in the Wild: Can only be caught in Europe, Rare

Flee Rate: Moderate

Capture Rate: High

Max CP: 1494

Best Basic Moves: Zen Headbutt, Confusion

Best Charged Moves: Psychic, Psybeam

Comments and Fun Facts: Not a very good Pokémon in GO. Can only be caught in Europe. In Red & Blue you could trade for a Mr. Mime named Marcel. Marcel is homage to Marcel Marceau, a famous French mime that passed away in 2007.

#123 Scyther C

Type: Bug / Flying

Evolves Into: Scizor in Generation II

Rarity in the Wild: Extremely Rare

Flee Rate: Moderate

Capture Rate: Moderate

Max CP: 2074

Best Basic Moves: Fury Cutter, Steel Wing

Best Charged Moves: Bug Buzz, X-Scissor

Comments and Fun Facts: Just an average Pokémon in GO. But maybe its evolution, Scizor, will be better in Generation II.

#124 Jynx C

Type: Ice / Psychic

Evolves Into: Does Not Evolve

Rarity in the Wild: Extremely Rare

Flee Rate: Moderate

Capture Rate: Moderate

Max CP: 1717

Best Basic Moves: Frost Breath, Pound

Best Charged Moves: Psyshock, Ice Shock

Comments and Fun Facts: Not all that great of a Pokémon in GO. Jynx are thought to pay homage to "Zwarte Piet". Zwarte Piet, a poor Moor from Spain, is part of the annual feast of St. Nicholas, celebrated in December in the Netherlands when sweets and presents are distributed to children. He dates back to 1850. Jynx can be frequently seen in a Santa's helper outfits.

#125 Electabuzz C

Type: Electric

Evolves Into: Electivire in Generation IV

Rarity in the Wild: Extremely Rare

Flee Rate: Moderate

Capture Rate: Moderate

Max CP: 2119

Best Basic Moves: Thunder Shock, Low Kick

Best Charged Moves: Thunder, Thunderbolt

Comments and Fun Facts: Not a great Pokémon in GO right now, but if you catch one early, you can use it as an attacking Electric Pokémon until you obtain Raichu or Jolteon.

#126 Magmar B+

Type: Fire

Evolves Into: Magmortar in Generation IV

Rarity in the Wild: Extremely Rare

Flee Rate: Moderate

Capture Rate: Moderate

Max CP: 2265

Best Basic Moves: Ember, Karate Chop

Best Charged Moves: Fire Blast, Flamethrower, Fire Punch

Comments and Fun Facts: A very good Fire Pokémon for attacking Gyms, it's just hard to find enough to power him up to max level.

#127 Pinsir C

Type: Bug

Evolves Into: Does Not Evolve

Rarity in the Wild: Extremely Rare

Flee Rate: Moderate

Capture Rate: Moderate

Max CP: 2122

Best Basic Moves: Fury Cutter, Rock Smash

Best Charged Moves: X-Scissor, Submission

Comments and Fun Facts: Not a very good Pokémon in GO right now. Pinsir is based on stag beetles that are commonly used in insect fighting – the creator of Pokémon was a bug collector after all! Pinsir is kind of a parallel to Scyther. Both are Bug Type. Pinsir was exclusive to Pokémon Blue, while Scyther was exclusive to Pokémon Red.

#128 Tauros C

Type: Normal

Evolves Into: Does Not Evolve

Rarity in the Wild: Found only in North America, Rare

Flee Rate: Moderate

Capture Rate: Moderate

Max CP: 1845

Best Basic Moves: Tackle, Zen Headbutt

Best Charged Moves: Earthquake, Horn Attack

Comments and Fun Facts: In the anime, Ash captured Tauros in an episode titled: "The Legend of Dratini". This episode was banned in many countries outside of Japan due to the use of guns. This lead to confusion for many viewers, because they had no idea how Ash got a Tauros.

#129 Magikarp F

Type: Water

Evolves Into: Gyarados (400 candies)

Rarity in the Wild: Uncommon

Flee Rate: High

Capture Rate: Very High

Max CP: 263

Best Basic Moves: Splash

Best Charged Moves: Struggle

Comments and Fun Facts: Magikarp's "Splash" attack is a mistranslation of the Japanese word "hop". That's why the attack animation is a hop. It's also why the attack is a normal attack not a water attack. The Magikarp plan: farm 101 Magikarp, run the IV checker and pick the best one, turn the rest into candy, and Evolve it into the dreaded Gyarados.

#130 Gyarados A-

Type: Water / Flying

Evolves Into: Does Not Evolve

Rarity in the Wild: Extremely Rare

Flee Rate: Low

Capture Rate: Very Low

Max CP: 2689

Best Basic Moves: Dragon Breath, Bite

Best Charged Moves: Hydro Pump, Dragon Pulse

Comments and Fun Facts: Gyarados is an excellent water Pokémon to use when attacking Gyms. Not that great of a Gym defender though.

#131 Lapras A+

Type: Water / Ice

Evolves Into: Does Not Evolve

Rarity in the Wild: Extremely Rare

Flee Rate: Moderate

Capture Rate: Moderate

Max CP: 2981

Best Basic Moves: Ice Shard, Frost Breath

Best Charged Moves: Ice Beam, Blizzard, Dragon Pulse

Comments and Fun Facts: Lapras is considered one of the best Gym defenders in Pokémon GO right now. High hit points, and it is very difficult to dodge his Blizzard attack.

#132 Ditto C-

Type: Normal

Evolves Into: Does Not Evolve

Rarity in the Wild: Not available

Flee Rate: High

Capture Rate: Moderate

Max CP: 920

Best Basic Moves: Pound

Best Charged Moves: Struggle

Comments and Fun Facts: Some folks believe that Ditto is a failed attempt at cloning Mew. Both have no gender. They have the same height and weight. Both can transform in the RPG. Both can use attacks of every other Pokémon in the RPG. Ditto is also found at the Mansion on Cinnabar Island where Mew cloning experiments were conducted.

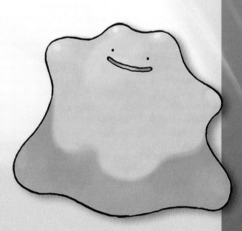

#133 Eevee D

Type: Normal

Evolves Into: Jolteon, Vaporeon, Flareon (25 candies each) in Generation I. Other Generations: Espeon, Umbreon, Sylveon, Glaceon, Leafeon

Rarity in the Wild: Uncommon

Flee Rate: High

Capture Rate: High

Max CP: 1077

Best Basic Moves: Tackle, Quick Attack

Best Charged Moves: Body Slam, Dig

Comments and Fun Facts: In general, you can't control how Eevee will evolve. However, once (and only once) you can choose which evolution you get by nicknaming your Eevee after one of the Eevee Brothers from the anime (Pyro = Flareon, Sparky = Jolteon, Rainer = Vaporeon). Eevee will probably evolve into several more different Pokémon in the upcoming years. So keep finding good IV Eevees if you plan to play this game in the future.

#134 Vaporeon A+

Type: Water

Evolves Into: Does Not Evolve

Rarity in the Wild: Extremely Rare

Flee Rate: Low

Capture Rate: Low

Max CP: 2816

Best Basic Moves: Water Gun

Best Charged Moves: Water Pulse, Hydro Pump, Aqua Tail

Comments and Fun Facts: One of the best all-around Pokémon in GO. Has the 4th highest HP and very good attacks.

#135 Jolteon B-

Type: Electric

Evolves Into: Does Not Evolve

Rarity in the Wild: Extremely Rare

Flee Rate: Low

Capture Rate: Low

Max CP: 2140

Best Basic Moves: Thundershock

Best Charged Moves: Thunder, Thunderbolt, Discharge

Comments and Fun Facts: Not as good as Vaporeon overall, but will make a good attacker when you need to attack a Gym with Electric Pokémon.

#136 Flareon

Type: Fire

Evolves Into: Does Not Evolve

Rarity in the Wild: Extremely Rare

Flee Rate: Low

Capture Rate: Low

Max CP: 2643

Best Basic Moves: Ember

Best Charged Moves: Flamethrower, Fire Blast, Heat Wave

Comments and Fun Facts: A solid Pokémon you can stick in Gyms as a defender, or as a fire-based attacker.

#137 Porygon C

Type: Normal

Evolves Into: Porygon2 in Generation II, and then Porygon Z in Generation IV

Rarity in the Wild: Extremely Rare

Flee Rate: Moderate

Capture Rate: Moderate

Max CP: 1692

Best Basic Moves: Tackle, Quick Attack

Best Charged Moves: Psybeam, Signal Beam, Discharge

Comments and Fun Facts: Not all that great of a Pokémon in GO right now, but might eventually be with future evolutions. Keep your best one or two handy, and ditch the rest.

#138 Omanyte D

Type: Rock / Water

Evolves Into: Omastar (50 candies)

Rarity in the Wild: Rare

Flee Rate: Moderate

Capture Rate: High

Max CP: 1120

Best Basic Moves: Water Attack, Mud Shot

Best Charged Moves: Ancient Power, Brine

Comments and Fun Facts: Based on an extinct mollusk called an Ammonite. Ammonites became extinct about 66 million years ago from the same event that made the last dinosaurs go extinct.

#139 Omastar

Type: Rock / Water

Evolves Into: Does Not Evolve

Rarity in the Wild: Extremely Rare

Flee Rate: Low

Capture Rate: Low

Max CP: 2234

Best Basic Moves: Rock Throw, Water Gun

Best Charged Moves: Rock Slide, Hydro Pump, Ancient Power

Comments and Fun Facts: A solid all-around Pokémon for attacking and defending Gyms.

#140 Kabuto *D*

Type: Rock / Water

Evolves Into: Kabutops (50 candies)

Rarity in the Wild: Rare

Flee Rate: Moderate

Capture Rate: High

Max CP: 1105

Best Basic Moves: Scratch, Mud Shot

Best Charged Moves: Ancient Power, Aqua Jet

Comments and Fun Facts: Based on an extinct trilobite that lived on the earth about 500 million years ago.

#141 Kabutops

Type: Rock / Water

Evolves Into: Does Not Evolve

Rarity in the Wild: Extremely Rare

Flee Rate: Very Low

Capture Rate: Low

Max CP: 2130

Best Basic Moves: Mud Shot, Fury Cutter

Best Charged Moves: Stone Edge, Water Pulse

Comments and Fun Facts: A pretty good attacker when Rock/Water is needed in battle.

#142 Aerodactyl

Type: Rock / Flying

Evolves Into: Does Not Evolve

Rarity in the Wild: Extremely Rare

Flee Rate: Moderate

Capture Rate: Moderate

Max CP: 2165

Best Basic Moves: Bite, Steel Wing

Best Charged Moves: Hyper Beam, Iron Head

Comments and Fun Facts: It can Mega-Evolve in the video games. If that ever comes to fruition in GO, Aerodactyl might become a force to be reckoned with in the future.

#143 Snorlax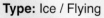

Type: Normal

Evolves Into: Does Not Evolve

Rarity in the Wild: Extremely Rare

Flee Rate: Moderate

Capture Rate: Moderate

Max CP: 3113

Best Basic Moves: Zen Headbutt, Lick

Best Charged Moves: Hyper Beam, Body Slam, Earthquake

Comments and Fun Facts: He is both an excellent Gym attacker and Gym defender. He has the 2nd highest HP in GO right now. Good luck finding a good one though, and then powering it up!

#144 Articuno A+

Type: Ice / Flying

Evolves Into: Does Not Evolve

Rarity in the Wild: Not available

Flee Rate: High

Capture Rate: Cannot be captured in the wild

Max CP: 2978

Best Basic Moves: Frost Breath

Best Charged Moves: Blizzard, Ice Beam, Icy Wind

Comments and Fun Facts: The names of all three Legendary Birds end in Spanish numbers.

#145 ZAPDOS A+

Type: Electric / Flying

Evolves Into: Does Not Evolve

Rarity in the Wild: Not available

Flee Rate: High

Capture Rate: Cannot be captured in the wild

Max CP: 3114

Best Basic Moves: Thundershock

Best Charged Moves: Thunder, Thunderbolt, Discharge

Comments and Fun Facts: A Legendary Bird that has never landed on its feet in an official image. It's airborne in all official images.

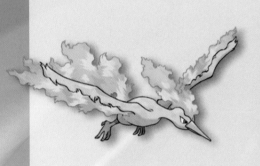

#146 MOLTRES A+

Type: Fire / Flying

Evolves Into: Does Not Evolve

Rarity in the Wild: Not available

Flee Rate: High

Capture Rate: Cannot be captured in the wild

Max CP: 3240

Best Basic Moves: Ember

Best Charged Moves: Fire Blast, Flamethrower, Heat Wave

Comments and Fun Facts: Rumor has it that you will somehow be able to obtain a Legendary Bird Pokémon based on the Team you chose at level 5. Nothing official as of this writing.

CP207

Dratini

HP 34 / 34

Dragon
Type

3.21 kg
Weight

1.83 m
Height

#147 DRATINI D

Type: Dragon

Evolves Into: Dragonair (25 candies)

Rarity in the Wild: Rare

Flee Rate: Moderate

Capture Rate: High

Max CP: 983

Best Basic Moves: Dragon Breath

Best Charged Moves: Aqua Tail, Wrap

Comments and Fun Facts: What a lovely sight to see when Pokémon hunting. Don't take any chances here. Use a Razz Berry and your very best Pokéball if you happen upon one.

#148 Dragonair

Type: Dragon

Evolves Into: Dragonite (100 candies)

Rarity in the Wild: Extremely Rare

Flee Rate: Low

Capture Rate: Very Low

Max CP: 1748

Best Basic Moves: Dragon Breath

Best Charged Moves: Dragon Pulse

Comments and Fun Facts: The Gym Leader Clair, a Dragon-type Master, uses a Dragonair in the video games and in the anime.

#149 Dragonite A+

Type: Dragon / Flying

Evolves Into: Does Not Evolve

Rarity in the Wild: Extremely Rare

Flee Rate: Very Low

Capture Rate: Very Low

Max CP: 3500

Best Basic Moves: Steel Wing, Dragon Breath

Best Charged Moves: Dragon Pulse, Dragon Claw, Hyper Beam

Comments and Fun Facts: Maybe the very best all-around Pokémon in GO right now. A fantastic Gym defender and attacker. Have fun tracking down all those Dratinis!

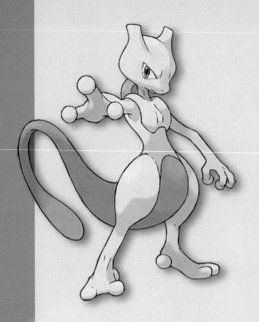

#150 Mewtwo A+

Type: Psychic

Evolves Into: Does Not Evolve

Rarity in the Wild: Not Available

Flee Rate: High

Capture Rate: Cannot be captured in the wild

Max CP: 4145

Best Basic Moves: Psycho Cut, Confusion

Best Charged Moves: Hyper Beam, Psychic, Shadow Ball

Comments and Fun Facts: Mewtwo is a genetic clone of Mew. Mewtwo is considered the strongest Pokémon in existence. His Mega Evolution in Generation VI gives him the strongest base statistics in the Pokémon RPGs. (Mega Evolutions are temporary, and can only occur during battles). In the Pokémon GO announcement trailer, a crowd is seen battling Mewtwo in Times Square in New York City. We wonder if that's an indicator on how he will be distributed?

#151 Mew A+

Type: Psychic

Evolves Into: Does Not Evolve

Rarity in the Wild: Not Available

Flee Rate: High

Capture Rate: Cannot be captured in the wild

Max CP: 3299

Best Basic Moves: Pound

Best Charged Moves: Psychic

Pojo's Pokémon Rating: A+

Comments and Fun Facts: Mew is thought to hold the DNA of all Pokémon, and be the ancestor of all Pokémon. He is generally not available for capture in the Role Playing Games. He is usually given away through special distribution events. We assume Mew will be given away in a Special Event in Pokémon GO too.